TOP
SECRET
FILES

THE CIVIL
WAR

TOP SECRET FILES

THE CIVIL WAR

STEPHANIE BEARCE

PRUFROCK PRESS INC.
WACO, TEXAS

Library of Congress Cataloging-in-Publication Data

Bearce, Stephanie.
  Top secret files : the Civil War : spies, secret missions, and hidden facts from the Civil
War / by Stephanie Bearce.
     pages cm
  Includes bibliographical references and index.
  ISBN 978-1-61821-250-4 (pbk. : alk. paper)
  1. United States--History--Civil War, 1861-1865--Secret service--Juvenile literature.
  2. United States--History--Civil War, 1861-1865--Underground movements--Juvenile
literature. 3. Spies--United States--History--19th century--Juvenile literature. 4. Spies-
-Confederate States of America--Juvenile literature. I. Title. II. Title: Spies, secret missions, and hidden facts from the Civil War.
  E608.B37 2014
  973.7'86--dc23
                        2014018526

Edited by Lacy Compton

Cover and layout design by Raquel Trevino

Background cover image courtesy of the Missouri Division of Tourism

ISBN-13: 978-1-61821-250-4

At the time of this book's publication, all facts and figures cited are the most current
available. All telephone numbers, addresses, and website URLs are accurate and active.
All publications, organizations, websites, and other resources exist as described in the
book, and all have been verified. The author and Prufrock Press Inc. make no warranty
or guarantee concerning the information and materials given out by organizations or
content found at websites, and we are not responsible for any changes that occur after
this book's publication. If you find an error, please contact Prufrock Press Inc.

Prufrock Press Inc.
P.O. Box 8813
Waco, TX 76714-8813
Phone: (800) 998-2208
Fax: (800) 240-0333
http://www.prufrock.com

TABLE OF CONTENTS

SECRETS

SPIES

SPECIAL MISSIONS

SECRET WEAPONS

SECRET FORCES

SECRETS

THE PLOT
AGAINST LINCOLN

Railroad baron Samuel Felton knew a terrible secret—one that could change the course of history. Felton had learned of a secret plot to assassinate **Abraham Lincoln** before he could be sworn in as President of the **United States of America**.

As the president of the Philadelphia, Wilmington and Baltimore Railroad, Samuel Felton had informants working for him to warn him about possible train robberies. But one informant brought news of a scheme to use the railroad to kill the president-elect. Abraham Lincoln was traveling by train from his home in Springfield, IL, to his inauguration in Washington. Along the way, Lincoln would make stops and speak at several cities. It was the perfect chance for Southern rebels to get rid of the man they hated. All they would have to do was blow up a bridge as Lincoln's train crossed over. It would be the end of a president who wanted to keep the states united, and it would throw the country into chaos.

There was only one man Samuel Felton could turn to for help. He sent an urgent letter to Allan Pinkerton, the head of the Pinkerton National Detective Agency. Allan Pinkerton was already a famous name in America. His detective agency had solved numerous bank robberies, train robberies, and murders. He had worked with Samuel Felton to catch train robbers and had also worked with Lincoln when he was a lawyer in Illinois. He was trusted by both men.

Pinkerton was working late in his Chicago office when a delivery boy handed him Felton's letter. The wording was mysterious and vague. Felton couldn't risk anyone reading his letter. But Pinkerton trusted his friend, and when he read the words, "I believe this matter to be extremely grave, not just for PW&B (railroad) but for the country as well," Pinkerton sent a three-word telegram back to Philadelphia: COMING AT ONCE.

In a private meeting, Felton told Pinkerton about the rumors that were circulating and that they seemed to center on Baltimore, MD. Baltimore was known to be an area especially sympathetic to Southern citizens who wanted their states to leave the United States. These citizens wanted individual states to decide their own laws, including laws about slavery.

Felton asked Pinkerton if he could find out the truth and protect president-elect Lincoln. Pinkerton agreed to take the job and immediately sent four of his best operatives.

Agent Timothy Webster arrived alone in a small town just north of Baltimore. He was dressed in the fine clothes of a Southern gentleman and had the assignment of infiltrating one of the secret militias of the area. He was to report back every detail of the militia's plans.

Harry Davies was sent to the city of Baltimore disguised as a sophisticated Frenchman who was sympathetic to the views of the Southern slave holders. He was a detective who could speak multiple languages and was a master of disguise.

That same day, agent Kate Warne was dressed in hoop skirts and a fine lace bonnet and introduced as a Southern belle visiting the beautiful city of Baltimore. She checked into a fancy hotel and began spying at every high-class party in the city.

Detective Allan Pinkerton disappeared from his Chicago office for a few days, but reappeared in Baltimore disguised as a man named Hutchinson. He rented a brand new office and waited for the reports to come in.

They were worse than Pinkerton had expected. A few nights after the agents had begun their assignments, Timothy Webster reported in to the Baltimore office. Pinkerton listened while Webster told about the plan he had overheard. On February 23, when Mr. Lincoln was passing through Maryland, members of a secret militia would attempt to assassinate him.

Pinkerton wanted more details. Webster told him that the headquarters for the planning of the assassination was a militia in Baltimore. The other militias were to wait for a telegraph signal after Lincoln was killed. Once they had received the signal, they were to attack by blowing up bridges and railroads and cutting telegraph lines. Webster finished his report and left immediately. He wanted to get back before sunrise so no one would suspect him of spying. Pinkerton told him to keep

THE PRIVATE EYE

Allan Pinkerton started one of the first legitimate private detective agencies in America. His company logo —the "All Seeing Eye"— ultimately influenced the phrase "private eye."

in close contact and to try to join the militia if he could. Then, Pinkerton sent the information to his other agents.

A few days later, Harry Davis was invited to join a secret militia in Baltimore. He snuck away to consult with Pinkerton and ask his advice. Davies knew that if he joined the militia he would have to swear an allegiance to the South and he did not want to be known as a traitor.

Pinkerton assured him that working undercover to save the president would not be considered treason, and Davies agreed to take the oath. It was a lucky thing he did, because the very night Davies took the oath, the leader of the militia explained their glorious plan for setting the South free from the rule of the Union. They would send eight assassins from their militia to kill the president-elect. With eight men ready to shoot, one of them would surely succeed.

The plan was to wait for Lincoln to get off the train in Baltimore and board a carriage to the hotel. That would be the point where the president would be most vulnerable. Once the plan was explained, all of the men in the militia lined up to pull a slip of paper from a jar. If the paper had a red dot, that man was to be one of the assassins.

Davies was sweating as he stood in line. What if he pulled a paper with a red dot? Would his cover be blown? Would he be allowed to leave and report back to Pinkerton? Davies nervously opened his paper. It was blank. As soon as the meeting was over, Davies reported back to his boss. Their next job was to warn the president.

Kate Warne was dressed in her finest and seated in the elegant Astor House in New York. In her bag was a letter addressed to Norman Judd, Lincoln's assistant. It was an urgent message from both Allan Pinkerton and Samuel Felton telling of the terrible assassination plot.

It wasn't until late in the afternoon that Judd had time to receive Miss Warne, who handed him the sealed envelope and explained that the information was so sensitive that Pinkerton could not trust either the mail or the telegraph. Judd read the note carefully and was convinced that he needed to meet with Pinkerton. He left immediately for Baltimore.

During the meeting in Baltimore, Pinkerton outlined a plan to fool the assassins and get the president safely to his inauguration. It would take the help of Pinkerton's best detectives, the cooperation of both the railroad and telegraph companies and the permission of Abraham Lincoln—the hardest one to convince.

The president-elect was well aware of how much conflict there was between the Northern and Southern states. He

PRESIDENTIAL SOLDIERS

Three men who would eventually **serve as President** of the United States fought in the Civil War: Ulysses S. Grant, Rutherford B. Hayes, and **William McKinley** (pictured). All of them fought on the side of the **Union**.

believed that by stopping in Baltimore and speaking to the people, he could help convince them that keeping the union together was a good idea. Lincoln felt that if he didn't stop there, he would be accused of being a coward and look like a weak leader. It took a lot of talking, but finally Lincoln agreed to a compromise. He would give the speech he had promised to deliver in Philadelphia and then he would allow Pinkerton to implement his plan.

After Lincoln gave his speech, it was announced that the president-elect had a terrible headache and would retire early for the evening. In reality, Kate Warne smuggled Lincoln onto a waiting train, and under armed guard, the train went directly to Washington.

All along the railroad, Pinkerton agents guarded bridges and overpasses so no militia could get near. And for safety's sake, some of the Pinkerton men even cut the telegraph lines so no one could alert the press that the president was ill.

The next morning, an astonished Washington woke up to find that Abraham Lincoln was already in town. When the residents of Baltimore found out that Lincoln had skipped his visit in their town, the people and the militia rioted, but Lincoln was unharmed.

Abraham Lincoln was sworn into office on March 4, 1861. A little more than a month later, on April 12, the South declared war. Lincoln hired Allan Pinkerton and his company to work as spies for the Union. Throughout the war, Pinkerton's men and women worked behind Southern lines to give information to Lincoln and the Union soldiers. For 4 years, Abraham Lincoln worked tirelessly to bring the Union back together. He succeeded, and on April 9, 1865, the Civil War ended.

Six days later Abraham Lincoln tried to relax and watch a play. Unfortunately, it was not a Pinkerton man who was assigned to guard the president. Lincoln was assassinated by John Wilkes Booth on April 15, 1865.

THE BLACK DISPATCH

Code-named "Contraband," a group of Black Americans who had been held as slaves and escaped to the North during the Civil War provided some of the most important spy information of the war.

The name *contraband* came about because one slave owner demanded that the Union Army return his slaves who had escaped to the North. Major General Benjamin Butler said that because Virginia had seceded from the Union, they were under no obligation to return slaves and the slaves were free to go their own way. Southern slave holders violently disagreed and argued that the slaves were contraband—illegal gains of war. From that point on, the escaped slaves were called "Contraband."

Many of the slaves who escaped during the war actively sought out Union Army officials to tell them about the information they had learned as they traveled north. This information became known as the "Black Dispatch" and was highly regarded by Union officers as being reliable and valuable.

Some of the former slaves were recruited by the Union to work as trained agents. They risked their lives and their new-found freedom to go undercover and return to the South as spies. One of these men was George Scott. He crossed through the Union line to freedom at Ft. Monroe, VA. As soon as he arrived, he told officers about the Southern military buildup. Scott volunteered to lead soldiers back to the South so they could witness for themselves what was going on. He successfully led several scouting groups and narrowly missed being killed by Confederate bullets.

Another valuable Black Dispatch came from W. H. Ringgold. He had been forced to work on a Confederate riverboat moving troop supplies up and down the York River in Virginia. For 6 months, he quietly did his job and at the same time memorized troop movements and army information. When a storm battered and damaged the steamboat, Ringgold managed to get away and headed straight for Baltimore and the Union Army. The officers in Baltimore soon realized that Ringgold had vital information, and they sent him directly to Allan Pinkerton in Washington. There, Ringgold was able to inform Pinkerton about the location of artillery batteries, troop concentrations, and the entire Confederate defense on the York River. General McClellan used Ringgold's information to plan a successful attack on the Virginia Peninsula.

Mary Touvestre was a freed slave who worked as a housekeeper for a navy engineer in Norfolk, VA. Her employer ignored Touvestre and did not consider her a threat of any kind. He talked openly about the amazing new ship he was building; a boat that was covered in iron and could resist all of the Union attacks.

FREDERICK DOUGLASS

Frederick Douglass was a former slave who became a vocal abolitionist. He gave speeches across America calling for the end of slavery. He also advocated for a woman's right to vote and equal rights for immigrants.

Touvestre knew this was information the Union needed to know. One night she snuck into the engineer's office and stole a set of the plans for the ironclad ship, the Merrimack. She immediately left for Washington. When Touvestre arrived, she had to convince the Navy officers that she was carrying important secret documents, but one look at the stolen plans, and the officers knew she had something big. Because of Touvestre's spy work, the Union accelerated their work on their own ironclad—the Monitor.

There were numerous other men and women who made significant contributions to the Union's spy data. The information the Union received from the Black Dispatches was the most productive of all the intelligence gathering of the war. The famous abolitionist Frederick Douglass wrote,

> The true history of this war will show that the loyal army found no friends at the South so faithful, active, and daring in their efforts to sustain the government as the Negroes. Negroes have repeatedly threaded their way through the lines of the rebels exposing themselves to bullets to convey important information to the loyal army of the Potomac.

Frederick Douglass, circa 1879

CONFEDERATE SIGNAL CORPS

Secret signals are a part of war. It's important to be able to tell soldiers what to do and keep it a secret from the enemy. The Confederate Army realized this and formed the Confederate Signal Corps. Their job was to keep communications SECRET!

During the Civil War, there were no telephones, no radios, and definitely no satellites. What did exist were telescopes, the electric telegraph, and flags. The Signal Corps used all of these and a few other communication tools.

Flags were inexpensive and easy to carry and became a standard way to send messages on the battlefield. The Signal Corps used a code called the wig-wag system, where waving the flag to the left, right, and front represented the numbers 1, 2, and 3, in that order. The message would be coded to the numbers. A signalman could wave the flag and several miles away another man would use a telescope to watch for the signal. He would immediately decode it, and get the message to the waiting officer. If signals needed to be sent at night, the signalmen used torches.

This is the alphabet, numbers, and code signals adopted late in the war:

A = 11	J = 2211	S = 121
B = 1221	K = 1212	T = 1
C = 212	L = 112	U = 221
D = 111	M = 2112	V = 2111
E = 21	N = 22	W = 2212
F = 1112	O = 12	X = 1211
G = 1122	P = 2121	Y = 222
H = 211	Q = 2122	Z = 1111
I = 2	R = 122	

To shorten the messages, certain words were assigned a letter. The following are a few examples:

A = Artillery	D = Center	G = Confederate
B = Back/retire	E = Return	H = Halt/stop
C = Cavalry	F = Forward	

And some phrases had their own flag signal assigned to them:

Phrase	Signal
I am ready	11211
Did you understand?	22
Error	Hold flag over head and parallel to ground
Message received and cease signaling	11, 11, 11, 3
End of word	3
End of sentence	33
End of message	333

Waving the flag so many times meant that the signal men had to be quite strong. And they had to work in all kinds of weather. Scorching heat, rain, sleet, or snow, the messages had to be sent.

As the war progressed, the Confederates had to keep changing their code system, as the Union soldiers became experts at decoding it. Messages were sent coded to words in books or rearrangements of the alphabet. But overall, the signal corps was a success.

The Confederate soldiers built tall towers so their signalmen could be seen from miles away. Unfortunately, their enemies could see them too and they became targets. It was one of the most dangerous jobs in the Confederate Army, with 1 in 12 signalmen being wounded or killed.

Flag signals were not the only form of communication they used. Members of the signal corps were also charged with conducting espionage. They were in charge of spying on the Union. They operated the "Secret Line," which was a human message passing system. Agents in mailrooms, shops, farmhouses, and restaurants hand-delivered coded letters from behind the enemy lines. Messages moved from Northern states like New York and Massachusetts down to the Southern capital of Richmond, VA. It was an efficient system, and when one person was caught or discovered, another volunteer immediately took his place.

The Confederate Signal Corps was disbanded in 1865 after the end of the Civil War.

SPY TRAINING

Secret Signals

You can practice sending secret signals just like the men of the Confederate Signal Corps.

Materials:
- ❏ A dark night
- ❏ Two flashlights
- ❏ Copy of the Confederate Signal Corps Alphabet
- ❏ A friend

Practice the CSC Alphabet with your friend in the house. Wave the flashlight to the left for 1. Wave it to the right for 2, and wave it in front for 3. After you have practiced inside, get the permission of adults to go outside at

night to send a real secret message. Station your friend far enough away from you that you cannot see his or her face in the dark. That way, you won't be able to "cheat" by mouthing the message.

Take turns sending a message. One person will flash the code and the receiver will watch and write down the message. Check with each other to see if you got the message right. Then, reverse roles. If you practice enough, you will be able to exchange light signal messages from a great distance.

SPY TRAINING

Spy Kit

Every spy needs a spy kit. What you put into it depends on your assignment, but there are a few essential ingredients that every spy needs.

❑ **Spy case:** You have to have some place to keep your spy tools and it needs to be portable. Do not simply label a shoebox "SPY TOOLS" and expect to be considered a professional! You need to be sneaky about how you store your tools. An old worn-out backpack is a good choice. It looks innocent enough, and it's lightweight for easy escapes. You could turn a reusable grocery bag into a spy case; just make sure your Mom doesn't try to use it for shopping! Anything can be used to hold your tools; just make sure it looks like something you would normally carry so it doesn't arouse suspicion.

❑ **Notebook and pencil:** You have to be able to take notes. Unless you have a photographic memory, you will forget something important. Write down the information; just make sure you keep it coded.

❏ **Magnifying glass:** A good magnifying glass is always useful. You can use it to look at fingerprints, read tiny messages, and check for clues.

❏ **Binoculars:** You need to be able to see what is going on in the distance. It may be the only way you can see the signals from your spy partner.

❏ **Sunglasses:** They aren't just to block out the sun; they are used to hide your face and eyes. There is a reason that you see pictures of spies wearing sunglasses. It works. A large pair of sunglasses can help you disguise your face. They can also disguise which way your eyes are looking. You can face one direction and move your eyes to look at something else without people suspecting that you are staring at them.

❏ **A hat:** Spies use hats because they work to help disguise their face. Just make sure you choose a hat that is not your favorite. You don't want people to recognize you because you have on your favorite team's hat!

You will find more tools to add to your spy kit, but these are the basics to get you started in the espionage game.

SPIES

SLAVE TURNED SPY

JOHN SCOBELL

John Scobell kicked his horse and urged him to go faster. He knew the Confederate soldiers were right behind, chasing them through the night. Scobell yelled at his spy partner, Hattie Lawton, to hurry. He'd seen the guns the Confederates were carrying. If they got within shooting distance, it would be five gunmen against two.

Suddenly, Scobell's horse stumbled and fell to the ground. Scobell went flying into a ditch. He scrambled to his feet, and Hattie turned her horse around to help him. Scobell's horse lay helpless on the road with a broken leg. Scobell knew there was no hope of them escaping with two people on Hattie's horse. He told Hattie she had to go on without him. The message for General McClellan had to be delivered. Hattie argued, but they both knew Scobell was right. Hattie reined her horse around and tore off to deliver the message.

Scobell pulled out his Smith & Wesson revolver and got ready to stand his ground. He waited until the first rebel was almost on top of him, then he stepped out from the cover of the bushes and took aim. His shot killed the rider's horse, and the soldier was thrown to the ground. Scobell fired again and hit the next soldier and he fell from his horse. Then he emptied his Smith & Wesson at the rest of the riders. When his gun was empty, Scobell dove behind the bushes and reloaded his gun. But there wasn't any need. The other riders turned their horses around and rode away.

Some time later, Scobell heard horses coming from the opposite direction. Hattie had made it to the general, who had sent the cavalry to rescue Scobell. They found him using torn strips of his shirt to bandage the men he had wounded.

Allan Pinkerton considered John Scobell to be one of the best spies under his direction, and he was the first Black spy hired by the U.S. government. Scobell was born a slave on a Mississippi plantation. His owner was unusual in his treatment of his slaves in that Scobell was educated beyond rudimentary reading and writing. He was taught to handle business documents and letters and was also a talented musician. When the war came, Scobell's owner gave his slaves their freedom.

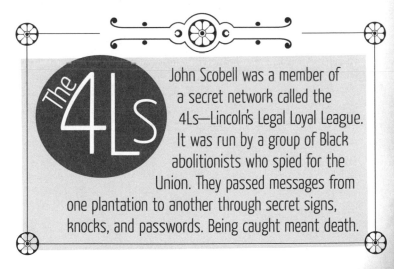

The 4Ls

John Scobell was a member of a secret network called the 4Ls—Lincoln's Legal Loyal League. It was run by a group of Black abolitionists who spied for the Union. They passed messages from one plantation to another through secret signs, knocks, and passwords. Being caught meant death.

Scobell immediately made his way north. There he met one of Allan Pinkerton's agents. Struck by his obvious intelligence, Pinkerton himself then interviewed Scobell.

Pinkerton realized that Scobell could be a great asset to the Union effort. The culture of the slave owners in the South meant that Black slaves and servants were often ignored. People talked openly in front of them and did not suspect that they might actually be spies for the North.

Scobell used this to great advantage. He often traveled from one Confederate camp to another dressed as a poor slave selling food or as a traveling entertainer. The men bought food from him or threw pennies to him when he was singing and playing his banjo. They never realized he was there counting battalions and weapons and memorizing troop movements. He sent messages back through an elaborate system of slaves and freedmen. Sometimes the information was so important that he had to deliver it in person.

At times, he played the part of a slave and accompanied Hattie Lawton. They were an excellent spy team. As a young woman, it was improper for Hattie to travel alone, but it was perfectly acceptable for her to be out riding accompanied by her "groom." Everywhere they traveled, Hattie talked and flirted with soldiers and society men while Scobell was getting information from the servants, slaves, and freedmen of the town.

Pinkerton trusted Scobell implicitly and actually had Scobell recruit additional spies for the Union. At the end of the war, McClellan and Pinkerton both agreed that the information they received from their Black agents, including Scobell, was invaluable.

SPY, SOLDIER, NURSE

SARAH EMMA EDMONDS

Sarah Emma Edmonds as "Frank Thompson"

Sarah Emma Edmonds was determined to serve her country, even if it meant disguising herself as a man.

During the Civil War, women were not allowed to serve in the army so Sarah cut off her hair and dressed in men's clothing. It took her four tries before she was accepted, but she was finally able to enlist. Lucky for Sarah, armies in the 1860s did not require a physical, so no one knew she was a girl.

Calling herself Frank Thompson, she started working as a male nurse in Virginia. Sarah (Frank) was an excellent nurse and worked tirelessly on the hospital wards, but she was always on the lookout for more adventure. When she heard that General McClellan's staff was looking for men to act as spies, Sarah volunteered.

The Brothers' War

Did you know that many historians refer to the Civil War as "a brothers' war"? It's for good reason—during the battle, many families were split as to their allegiances. Stories abound of fathers fighting against sons and brothers fighting against brothers. These stories usually end in tragedy, as roughly 620,000 men, or 2% of the population, is thought to have perished in the war.

Dressed as Frank Thompson, she answered questions on weapons, geography, and war tactics. Frank Thompson was immediately hired and given a mission to go behind the lines. Sarah had to come up with a new disguise. She decided to pose as a slave. She used silver nitrate to darken her skin and put on the ragged clothes of a slave. She was assigned work building the fortifications to protect against the Union. Her hands got so blistered that she switched jobs and worked the rest of the time in the kitchen.

The soldiers talked freely in front of the slaves, and soon Sarah learned about the weapon and ammunition supplies, the number of troops and plans for movement. She memorized all she had learned and snuck back across to the Union lines. Her information was so useful that she was sent back out to spy some more.

This time, Sarah disguised herself as a slave woman. She worked as a laundress washing Confederate soldiers' clothes. One day, a packet fell out of an officer's uniform. It was full of official papers, and Sarah knew she had a treasure trove of information. She left her laundry job and reported back to headquarters. Her superiors were delighted with her work. They had all sorts of plans for Frank Thompson.

Sarah went on numerous assignments as a spy. She played the role of an Irish peddler woman and a Southern gentleman. In between her assignments as a spy, she dressed as Frank Thompson and kept up her duties as a male nurse. No one ever suspected Sarah's secret, and she wanted to keep it that way. She didn't know how people would react if they knew she had been fooling them the whole time.

It worked fine until Sarah became sick with malaria. She knew she could not be treated at her own hospital, because her secret would be out. So she bought a train ticket and traveled to Cairo, IL, where she checked into a hospital there. When she was better and left the hospital, she found out that Frank Thompson was wanted by the law for deserting his post in the army. Sarah knew she couldn't go back as Frank. She spent the rest of the war serving as a nurse in Washington, DC, where she dressed as a woman.

After the war, Sarah wrote a book telling about her work as a spy and a nurse. It was a very popular book, and Sarah gave all the profits to the U.S. war relief fund. She met and married Linus Seelye and had three sons. One of her sons enlisted and served in the army—just like Mom did!

LA BELLE REBELLE

BELLE BOYD

Belle sat with her face pressed against the rough wood. She tried to keep her breathing slow and quiet as she peered through the knothole to watch the Yankee soldiers. No one could find out she was hiding in the room next to the men. If they found her spying again, she would surely be hanged.

The soldiers rolled open a map and began talking about where the troops would be moving. Belle stared at the map. She couldn't see all of it, but she could see enough to know where the troops were headed. Some of them were moving out of the area, leaving the remaining Northern troops vulnerable to attack. Belle knew she needed to get this information to Confederate Major General Stonewall Jackson; it could give the South an advantage in the battle.

She slipped quietly out of her hiding place and went back to her room in her aunt's boarding house. She had her maid dress her in a dark wool riding suit. It would be hot in the warm evening, but it would help Belle blend in with the shadows and the trees. Under cover of darkness, Belle saddled her horse and began the 15-mile ride to the Confederate soldiers' camp.

She kept her horse off the roads to avoid meeting any Yankee soldiers and rode through the woods and fields of the Shenandoah River Valley. At last, she could see the glow of the Confederate campfires and the outline of their tents. Belle was stopped by an armed guard, but she was used to dealing with soldiers. She had been spying since she was 17. She had learned how to hide guns in the hoops of her skirt and letters

DOUBLE AGENT WEBSTER

Timothy Webster was a double agent working for the Union. He was the first Civil War spy to be **executed** and had to be hanged twice because there was a problem with the rope the first time. Webster declared, "I suffer a double death" as he was hanged **the second time**.

in the heel of a shoe. She had been caught and held in prison, but nothing was going to make her stop spying for the South.

Belle jumped off her horse and informed the guard she had an important message for the Major General. After she had given her evidence to a staff officer, she leaped back on her horse and started home. She had to get back before morning or the Union soldiers staying at her aunt's boarding house would know she had informed on them.

Her nighttime ride was successful, and Major General Jackson and his troops were able to defeat the North in that skirmish. Belle had once again proved her worth as a teenage spy.

The soldiers usually felt that a young girl could not be any threat to them. She often flirted with and teased both the Union and Confederate soldiers. This was how she misled them into believing she was a girl only interested in flirtations and not in serious politics. It was why they released her from prison and why she was able to pass notes so easily. Union soldiers thought a teenage Southern girl could not possibly be trusted with any important information. But Belle was as excellent spy and was not only trusted to deliver messages and weapons, but also in making battle decisions.

When Belle later learned that Union soldiers were retreating from her town and planning to burn the bridges as they left, she actually ran to the battlefield. Grown men were running from the fight. Rifle shots rained around her, some coming so close they left holes in her long skirts. A mortar shell exploded in front of her and Belle dropped to the ground, but she quickly scrambled back to her feet and ran on toward the closest officer.

When she delivered her message, the officer offered her an escort back home, but Belle refused and said she would return the same way she came. She ran back through the fighting and made it safely home. The commander used her information to stop the Union soldiers from burning the bridges, and Belle received a letter of thanks from Stonewall Jackson.

Belle was arrested several times, but only spent a few weeks in prison. She was not a good prisoner. Held captive in in Old Capitol Prison in Washington, DC, she was often heard singing Southern fight songs out of her window. Her supporters devised a unique way of communicating with her. They used a bow and arrow to shoot a rubber ball into her window. Belle would sew messages inside the ball and throw them back outside.

Eventually Belle was convicted of espionage and was banished to the South. She tried to sail for England, but was again arrested. Later, she escaped to Canada and was eventually smuggled to England.

She lived in England for a while after the war. She married three times and tried her hand at acting, but nothing ever compared to the excitement she found being a spy for the Confederacy. She wrote an autobiography about her adventures in the war and told the stories onstage. Belle died as dramatically as she lived: She had a heart attack while performing the story of her life and died on the stage.

LIKE FATHER, LIKE SON

John and Charles Phillips were a father and son spy team who worked for the Union. **Charles was just 14** when he started spying. His cover was as a "newsboy" selling papers in the Southern city of **Richmond**. The team was quite successful, and Charles hand-delivered one message **directly to General Ulysses S. Grant.**

CRAZY BET

The woman shuffled down the streets of Richmond, VA, her torn skirt dragging in the dirt. A ragged bonnet barely covered her scraggly, uncombed hair. Children pointed and mothers told them, "Stay away from her. That's just poor Crazy Bet."

The woman smiled. Her plan was working. As long people thought she was crazy, they would ignore her and leave her alone. What a perfect cover for a spy!

Elizabeth Van Lew was neither poor nor crazy. She was born into a wealthy Southern family who paid for her to attend a private Quaker school in the North. When she graduated and returned home to Richmond, she became a vocal antislavery activist. When her father died, Elizabeth and her brother freed all of the slaves her family owned and helped many of them go to school and start their own businesses. She also used all of her inheritance of $10,000 (equivalent to $200,000 in today's money) to buy the relatives of her former slaves and then free them.

Concerned for their well-being, Elizabeth stayed in close contact with her former slaves and many of them considered Elizabeth a close personal friend. When the war broke out, several of the former slaves risked their lives and their freedom to return to the South and work with Elizabeth in her spy ring.

She started her work for the Union by offering food and help to the Union prisoners held at the Confederate prison in Richmond. With the help of gingerbread and buttermilk, she gained the confidence of prison commander Lieutenant David H. Todd (half-brother of Mary Todd Lincoln, the president's wife). Soon, she was able to come and go as she pleased. The guards became used to seeing her visit the prisoners and believed she was just a harmless woman. They talked freely in front of her and she started learning of information that might help the Union. Elizabeth sent notes to local commanders, who found that she was giving them accurate and valuable information. She was asked to send them all of the information she could learn.

Elizabeth set up an elaborate spy network. She realized that just as the soldiers had thought she was harmless as a woman and were willing to talk in front of her, they would act the same way around slaves or servants. Elizabeth asked some of her former slaves if they would be willing to help her spy on the Confederate Army. Many of them agreed, including Mary Bowser.

After Elizabeth had freed Mary, she sent Mary to school in the North and paid for her education. This smart, well-educated woman took on the difficult task of working as a spy inside the Confederate capital. Mary was hired as a servant in the household of Confederate President Jefferson Davis. She was able to listen in on conversations and read secret papers. She passed all of her information to Elizabeth Van Lew and her network of spies.

Messages were coded or written in invisible ink. One method Elizabeth used was to loan books to the Union prisoners. They would underline certain words in the books and when Elizabeth went to pick up the books, she would also pick up a message.

Once Elizabeth had a message, she had to get it from her house in Richmond to the front lines where the Union Army was fighting. She would send baskets of food to the general at the front line. The basket always contained some eggs—one of which was hollowed out and a slip of paper placed inside. Other times, messages were coded then sewn inside clothing or placed inside the heel of a shoe.

Elizabeth became a master of spycraft and taught her assistants well. Not one of her spy ring was ever caught. And after the war, General Grant declared that Elizabeth Van Lew had sent him "the most valuable information received from Richmond during the war."

In addition to working as a spy, Elizabeth also helped smuggle Union prisoners out of the South. She had hidden rooms built into her mansion and soldiers who managed to escape from the prison hid in the walls of her house until she could arrange for safe transport for them to the North. Several times her home was searched by suspicious Confederate soldiers, but they never found anyone hiding in her home.

But the price of being a spy was quite high. Elizabeth had used all of her money to free slaves and help the Union. After the war, she was penniless. In addition, all of her Richmond neighbors considered her a traitor to the South and would have nothing to do with her. She once wrote, "No one will walk with us on the street. No one will go with us anywhere; and it grows worse as the years roll on."

Not everyone had forgotten Elizabeth Van Lew and her courage and generosity—a group of wealthy Bostonians collected money and provided a small annuity to her in her old age as thanks for the service she had given to the Union.

She died in 1900, nearly 40 years after the start of the Civil War, but even then, the Southerners would not forgive her. There was no crowd at her funeral, and she was buried in an unmarked grave, which stayed that way until the family of Union Colonel Paul J. Revere heard of her death. He was one of the Union soldiers Elizabeth had helped escape from prison. The family had a solid granite marker made to commemorate her life.

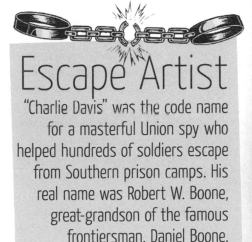

Escape Artist

"Charlie Davis" was the code name for a masterful Union spy who helped hundreds of soldiers escape from Southern prison camps. His real name was Robert W. Boone, great-grandson of the famous frontiersman, Daniel Boone.

WIDOW GREENHOW

FROM THE ORIGINAL NEGATIVE   BY BRADY
IN THE COLLECTION OF L C HANDY
WASHINGTON, DC

Rose O'Neal Greenhow was a grieving widow and a devoted mother of four children. She spent her days caring for her children, entertaining friends of her dead husband, and spying for the Confederate army.

Rose and her husband, Dr. Greenhow, were part of elite society in Washington, DC, and after his death she continued to host parties for prominent politicians, judges, and army officers. Her contacts with so many important people made her the perfect choice for a spy. Who would suspect a sweet widow and mother of spying?

Confederate Captain Thomas Jordan knew that Rose was a Southern sympathizer and one evening in 1861, he asked Rose if she would serve the South as a spy. Rose agreed and Jordan gave her a 26-figure cipher to use for coding messages and told her to send him dispatches of any information she could learn.

Captain Jordan had no idea how important Widow Greenhow's information would be. In July of 1861, Rose learned about the Battle of Bull Run. She sent information about the Union General's plans to Confederate General Beauregard. It ultimately helped the South win the battle. After the battle, Rose received a telegram that read, "Our President and our General direct me to thank you. We rely upon you for further information. The Confederacy owes you a debt."

Rose continued her spying, but after the Union defeat at Bull Run, Northern officers became suspicious that Rose was spying. Detective Allan Pinkerton was called in to investigate. Just one month after the Bull Run victory, Pinkerton and his detectives searched Rose's house and found evidence of her spying activities, including coded messages she had tried to burn. Rose was placed under house arrest and was guarded at all times by Pinkerton Detectives.

Pinkerton allowed Rose to have visitors in the hope of overhearing information that the Pinkerton Detectives could use to help the North. Rose knew what was going on and set up a signal system using the position of her window shades and the number of candles lit in her window to get messages to her fellow spies.

SPY AND FREEDOM FIGHTER

Harriet Tubman is famous for her work as a conductor on the **Underground Railroad**, where she helped lead hundreds of slaves to freedom. During the Civil War, she also **served as a spy** for the Union. She made regular trips to the South to get information and reported **back to Union officers.**

Because of this, she was moved to Old Capitol Prison. Before the war, the "prison" was a boarding house and was used during the Civil War to house political and some war prisoners. Rose was allowed to have her youngest daughter with her in prison. Eight-year-old "Little" Rose and her mother spent 5 months in the Old Capitol prison. In May of 1862, Rose was released without a trial on the condition that she live within Confederate boundaries. The Union officers believed that if they moved Rose out of Washington, DC, she would not be a great threat to the Union. They were wrong.

Once she was released from prison, Confederate President Jefferson Davis asked Rose to be a special courier to England. Her mission was to talk to the wealthy Southern sympathizers in England and raise money for the Confederate cause.

Rose spent 2 years in England. She went to France and was received in the court of Napoleon III. She had an audience with Queen Victoria and even got engaged to an English earl. In August of 1864, Rose needed to report back to the Confederacy. She boarded a ship for America carrying secret messages and $2,000 worth of gold. It was money she had earned selling a book about her experiences as a spy. She planned to donate the money to help the Southern cause.

As Rose's ship neared the shore, a Union gunboat spotted and began to chase it. Her ship ran aground near Wilmington, NC. Stranded, but close to the shore, Rose and some of her fellow crew members boarded a rowboat and attempted to row in to shore. The little boat was swamped with ocean water and overturned. No one could find Rose.

The next morning, her body washed ashore. Rose had drowned, pulled underwater by the weight of the gold she had sewn into her underwear and hidden in a pouch around her neck.

LAFAYETTE BAKER

The dark-haired man stood outside the tent of General Winfield Scott, yelling at the general's aide. He needed to see the general immediately—he had important information for the general's ears only. The man was so loud and so insistent that General Scott finally said to show him in.

Lafayette Baker introduced himself and told General Scott that he was an accomplished spy ready to give his services to the Union Army. The general was intrigued by Baker's daring and offered him an assignment. If Baker could go behind the Confederate lines and get information about the numbers of soldiers and pieces of artillery, Scott would give him a job. Baker boldly told the General it would be an easy assignment for a man with his experience.

What the General didn't know was that Baker had never worked as a spy. The closest he came to any spy or detective work was when he had helped with some law enforcement in San Francisco during the Gold Rush. But Baker was known to tell tall tales and told so many of them that people were never sure which stories were true—a skill that he put to good use as a spy.

Baker set out on his first assignment with the cover story of being a photographer. He purchased a tripod and a broken box camera, then confidently marched into Confederate camps and offered his services to photograph their officers and troops. The camera was a relatively new invention and both Union and Confederate soldiers often posed for pictures.

Baker was somewhat successful. He did get captured a couple of times and accused of being a spy, but he managed to tell stories and wrangle himself out of prison. After a few weeks, he returned to General Scott with the requested information. Scott hired him on the spot.

General Scott was so impressed with his new spy that he often bragged about him to other officers. When Secretary of War Edwin Stanton heard about Baker's success as a spy behind enemy lines, he hired Baker to be his personal secret agent.

Soon Baker was in charge of a large group of agents and detectives. One of their main goals was to find and interrogate people they believed were traitors to the Union. When they captured suspected traitors, they were taken to a prison in the old capitol building and questioned. The questioning was anything but gentle and Baker was sometimes accused of being too aggressive in his pursuit of traitors. He told everyone that his motto was "Death to Traitors" and he meant it.

One of his most famous prisoners was Belle Boyd. Although Baker kept her a prisoner for several weeks, Belle never confessed to spying and eventually Baker had to let her go. In her autobiography, Belle accused Baker of torturing her. The public was outraged—even if she was a spy, people did not want to hear about a teenage girl being tortured!

But Secretary Stanton received a great deal of useful information from Baker, so he wasn't going to get rid of him. Stanton often had Baker spy on other Union officers and friends of President Lincoln and report information that would help Secretary Stanton politically. Baker was rewarded by being named the head of the Union Intelligence Service.

Baker may have enjoyed spying a bit too much. He was caught spying on his boss. When Secretary Stanton found out that Baker was intercepting his personal telegraph messages, Baker was demoted and sent to work in New York. Baker argued that he was right to spy on Stanton because the secretary was plotting against the president. Baker was not able to prove his claims.

When President Lincoln was shot, Baker was working in New York, but Stanton called him back to help capture John Wilkes Booth. Baker and his agents tracked down the assassin and his assistants, and for his work, Baker was rewarded with a generous portion of the $100,000 reward.

But just a few months later, Baker was back in trouble. He was caught spying on the new leader, President Johnson, and was fired. Baker admitted that he was indeed spying, because Johnson and his cabinet were suppressing information about Lincoln's death. He said that he had found John Wilkes Booth's diary and that the Department of War was hiding information. Stanton finally did release the assassin's diary, but Baker said that pages were missing. Baker said he believed there was a conspiracy to murder Lincoln and that some politicians like Stanton were a part of the conspiracy.

Hearings were held, but Baker's claims were never proved. Baker was sure that he was right and publicly declared that he was afraid for his own life. Strangely, Baker did die soon after the hearings. Doctors said it was from meningitis, but in 1977, more than 100 years after his death, a professor from Indiana State University conducted tests on some of Baker's hair and said that Baker had been poisoned with arsenic!

Was Baker telling the truth or was it another one of his tall tales? History may never know the truth.

SOUTHERN SPY FOR THE NORTH

Phillip Henson was a friendly sort of fellow. Born and raised in Northeast Alabama, he had spent his youth traveling across the United States from Alabama through Kansas and on to New Mexico. He drove cattle, carried mail, and learned to love the American states and their union.

When the Civil War broke out in 1861, Henson was married and working in a country store in Mississippi. He did not want to be forced to serve as a soldier for the Confederacy, so he persuaded a local plantation farmer to hire him as the overseer. Overseers were exempt from Southern military service. Henson had to keep his loyalty to the Union a secret from his neighbors to protect his life and the life of his family.

When Grant invaded Mississippi near the end of 1862, Henderson may have been one of the few men who was actually happy to see the Union soldiers. He quickly took the oath

THE SPY SPEAKS

After his retirement from the secret service, Philip Henson traveled around the country giving speeches about his days as a spy. To help promote his tours he grew out his beard to amazing 6 feet and 3 inches. He claimed to have the "longest beard of any living man."

of allegiance to the Union, but unlike his neighbors, he took the oath because he wanted to, not because he was forced to. Henson believed in the Union and wanted the United States to stay together as a country.

Henson believed he could best serve the union as a spy and quickly volunteered. With his deep Southern drawl and unique ability to make friends everywhere, he became one of the Union's greatest spies behind the Confederate lines. When he was given the assignment of finding out about the Confederacy's strength in Vicksburg, MS, Henson came up with a simple but brilliant plan.

He saddled his horse and, with an extra horse in tow, rode north to visit one of his old friends, Jesse Johnsey. Johnsey was a devoted Southern Confederate and several of his seven sons were serving in Vicksburg. When Henson arrived, he offered Johnsey the extra horse and suggested that they take a ride to Vicksburg to check on "our boys." Never suspecting that his old acquaintance was a Northern spy, Johnsey accepted the kind offer and the two men set off to visit the Confederate stronghold.

Whenever the men met Confederate pickets (guards), Henson would offer them a swig of rye and tell them how happy he was to get to visit the boys. Henson spent several days in Vicksburg wandering around the town without anyone stopping him. He memorized troop numbers, city defenses, and weak spots. And after leaving his friend, Henson made his way back to the Union camp and reported all he had learned to Brigadier General Greenville Dodge. General Dodge was so impressed with the information that he gave Henson a fine black horse named Black Hawk.

For the next 2 years, Henson worked for General Dodge visiting different Confederate camps, offering swigs of his rye and talking about "our Southern boys." It wasn't until May of 1864 that Henson was captured and imprisoned as a Union spy. He spent months in horrific conditions. For some time, he was confined in a tiny windowless room called the sweatbox. Many men died in the sweatbox, but somehow Henson survived. Then, in February of 1865, he managed to escape and made his way back to General Dodge. Dodge was relieved to see his favorite spy, but simply said, "Well, Phil, the damn rope has not been made yet to hang you."

When President Lincoln was assassinated, General Grant hired Henson as a secret service agent and gave him the job of tracking down the truth about the assassination. For his service to his country, Grant awarded Henson the title of Lieutenant Colonel. Henson died in 1911 at the age of 84.

SPY TRAINING

Spy Fan

In Civil War times, there were no air conditioners and no electric fans. The women wore layers of petticoats and corsets. So you can imagine that in the summer, ladies got HOT. Because of this, it was common practice for women to carry hand fans. Some were elaborate fans made from silk, while others were simple paper fans.

It was also customary for gentlemen to pick up items that a lady dropped. If a woman dropped her handkerchief or fan, a gentleman would pick it up and hand it back to her. Spies took advantage of this custom by using fans to pass messages. A lady could write a message on a piece of paper and conceal it in her fan. Then she would drop it in front of the man to whom she needed to deliver the message. When he picked it up, he would pull out the note.

Another way was to write the message on the fan. Most of the fans had elaborate illustrations. The woman could hide the message in the drawings on the fan. Then, she would walk by her spy contact and drop the fan but keep moving. He would pick up the fan and give it back to her after he had read the message.

Materials:

- ❏ Two sheets of 8.5" x 11" paper
- ❏ Glue
- ❏ Stapler
- ❏ Markers or crayons
- ❏ Tape

First tape the two sheets of paper together on the short ends (8.5" ends). Then, color both sides of your fan. Make an elaborate design so that it is easy to hide words in the design. Once you have finished the design, write your message in the design.

Next, lay the paper lengthwise and fold it accordion style.

Staple one end of the paper together. Spread out the other end to form a fan.

Now, just wait for your opportunity to deliver your secret message.

Secret Eggs

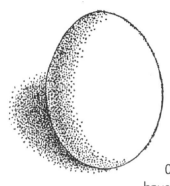

Do you wonder how Crazy Bet hid messages in eggs? Try out this project and you can make your own secret message eggs. This may require the help of an adult, so grab one and have some fun!

Materials:

- ☐ Uncooked eggs
- ☐ Small sharp nail
- ☐ Thin paper
- ☐ Pencil
- ☐ A clean bowl

Use the nail to bore a hole in each end of an uncooked egg. You will have to be careful. You can't just stab the shell, or it will break. Use the nail like a drill to make the holes. Wiggle the nail around to break up the yolk inside of the egg.

Once you have a hole on each end, put your lips around the hole on the larger end of the egg. Then blow hard until the white and yolk of the egg come out of the opposite hole. Catch the white and yolk in a clean bowl. You can use it to make omelets for supper or throw them into a cake mix.

After the egg is empty, set it aside to dry. This could take 24 hours.

Come back the next day, and write a message on the thin sheet of paper. Roll the message into a very tight scroll, then insert it through the hole in the egg. The message is hidden inside and can only be revealed by someone cracking the egg open.

Do you see why this was such a smart way to send messages?

SPECIAL MISSIONS

THE GREAT LOCOMOTIVE CHASE

Union General Ormsby Mitchel wanted to kidnap a train. Not just any train, but a train running on the Western and Atlantic Railroad. His plan was to hijack a train in the South, and as he drove it north, burn bridges, wreck tracks, and cut telegraph lines. This would cut off an important rail supply line to the South. Without essential food and clothing being shipped to the South, General Mitchel believed the Southerners would be starved into losing the war.

In the spring of 1862, General Mitchel put his plan into action. He sent Union raider John J. Andrews and a small band of men to Georgia. Disguised as civilians, they snuck through enemy territory and arrived at the train station in Marietta, GA. They bought tickets for a trip north and boarded a train pulled by a locomotive named *General*.

The raiders took their seats among the unsuspecting passengers and patiently waited until the first stop. There, all of

the other passengers got off the train to eat breakfast. The raiders stayed on the train pretending to nap or rest.

As soon as the last passenger stepped off, Andrews and his raiders leapt into action. They seized control of the locomotive and three train cars. They uncoupled the rest of the train and took off, leaving the passengers and crew screaming and yelling on the station platform.

The crew of the train knew immediately they had been fooled. Some of the men tried to run after the train. The conductor and some of his crew members jumped on a railroad handcar and furiously pumped to try to catch the Union hijackers and their locomotive.

After a few miles, the Union raiders stopped the locomotive and began to implement the next part of their plan. They cut the telegraph lines and tried to wreck the rails. But the raider's axes and hammers were no match for the strong steel of the train rails. The raiders didn't inflict much damage. They scrambled back on the locomotive and started up the engine.

By this time the conductor and his men had reached Adairsville, GA. There they got help from the men who drove a fast-moving locomotive called *Texas*. This locomotive was headed south, but the train engineer shifted into reverse and sent the locomotive hurtling up the railroad *backward* at the breakneck speed of 60 miles per hour. It was twice as fast as most trains went when driving forward.

The Union raiders heard the whistle of *Texas* and knew they had no more time to stop and destroy tracks. Andrews and his men set fire to two of the boxcars and cut them loose to slow down *Texas*.

But the Confederate crew was determined to get their locomotive back. They shoved the burning box cars onto a side track and kept chasing the *General* and its hijackers. The Confederates drove their locomotive backward for 80 miles before the *General* ran out of fuel.

Andrews and his raiders abandoned the locomotive and ran for cover in the nearby woods. Because the men were dressed as civilians, they knew they could be charged with espionage and killed. Andrews and his raiders were caught, but some of the men managed to escape from the local jail and made it back to the North. Five of the captured men were exchanged for Southern prisoners of war, but Andrews and seven others were hanged.

The train kidnapping was deemed a failure and was not tried again.

Mr. Lincoln's Beard

What makes Abraham Lincoln so memorable to most? His hat, yes, but also his beard! Did you know that until the last few weeks of the presidential election, Lincoln sported a clean-shaven face? He later arrived in Washington showing off his now-famous whiskers. It's said that 11-year-old Grace Bedell was the President's inspiration for growing his beard, after she wrote him a letter saying he would look better with one, adding that "All the ladies like whiskers," and suggesting that she'd promise to get her brothers to vote for him if he let his beard grow.

SNEAKY RETREAT

Everybody talks about sneak attacks, but at Fort Davidson, MO, it was a sneak retreat that saved the day.

Confederate General Sterling Price was determined to capture Fort Davidson as he marched toward St. Louis. Price had a grand scheme of marching into St. Louis and taking over the huge armory. With all of the guns and ammunition in St. Louis, he just knew he could win the war for the South. Tiny Fort Davidson was all that was in his way.

The Confederate soldiers attacked Fort Davidson on September 26, 1864. It was going to be an easy fight—the Confederates outnumbered the Union soldiers by nearly 10 to one. For 24 hours, the battle was furious. The Confederate soldiers were sure they were winning the fight and demanded the Union soldiers in the fort surrender. But Brigadier General Thomas Ewing Jr. refused.

Ewing knew the fight was hopeless. There were simply too many Confederate soldiers, but he was not about to surrender. Ewing had several Black civilians in his fort and he knew the Confederates would either kill them or enslave them. He was not going to just give them up to the Confederacy.

It would take a miracle and a daring plan to save the Union soldiers and civilians. Ewing had just the idea: On the night of September 27, the soldiers in the fort very quietly put all of their ammunition and equipment inside the building where they stored their gunpowder. They lit a very slow burning fuse and then the soldiers and civilians all snuck out of the fort. They had to move quietly between the campfires of the Confederate soldiers, but not one person was captured. And none of the Confederates saw the soldiers leave the fort. Later that night, a huge explosion rocked the area.

As soon as it was daylight, the Confederates stormed the fort only to find it completely empty. The weapons had all been destroyed and there was not a living person present. General Price was furious. He had spent 2 days in battle and had captured an abandoned fort. He never did march into St. Louis and was eventually defeated near Kansas City.

Ewing received a personal thank you from a grateful President Lincoln. His idea of a sneaky retreat had made headlines throughout the country and had totally embarrassed the Confederacy. It was a very successful retreat!

OPERATION DABNEY

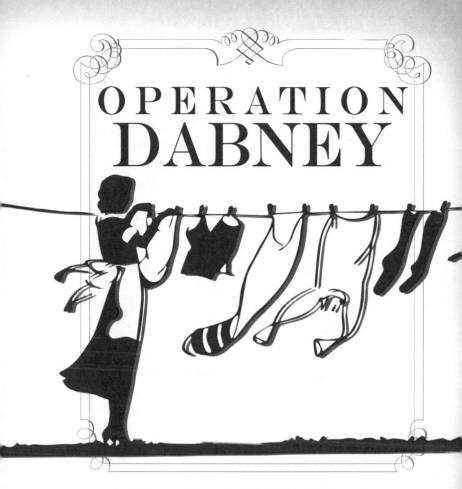

Confederate Generals A.P. Hill and James Longstreet were baffled. Every move they made, the Union was there. It seemed like someone knew all of their plans. There had to be a traitor in the ranks. But after a thorough investigation, they still had no idea who was acting as a spy and how they were getting the information to the Union. That's because they never investigated Mrs. Dabney, a quiet Black servant who simply hung out the laundry every day. She was the spy.

The Dabneys were a free Black couple who volunteered their services to the Union Army stationed on the banks of the Rappahannock River in Fredericksburg, VA. Their plan was simple and extremely effective.

Mr. Dabney went to work for the Union Army as a cook and a groom. His wife went across the river and obtained work at the Confederate camp as the laundress. The Confederate soldiers never paid any attention to Mrs. Dabney and talked freely in front of her. As soon as she learned of a battle plan or troop movement, she went to her clothesline and hung up the laundry.

Across the river, her husband watched the clothesline for the messages from his wife. A gray shirt was used to represent General Longstreet and a white shirt represented General Hill. Moving the shirts on the clothesline told Mr. Dabney which direction each general was going with his troops. If one of the shirts was removed from the clothesline, it meant that general was headed into Richmond (the capitol of the Confederate government) to get new orders.

Different colored shirts and blankets represented different officers and their troops. It was an elaborate code system that only the Dabneys understood. But it worked—Mrs. Dabney was never suspected as a spy and as long as Generals Hill and Longstreet were camped at Fredericksburg, Mr. Dabney was able to tell the Union Army every move they planned to make.

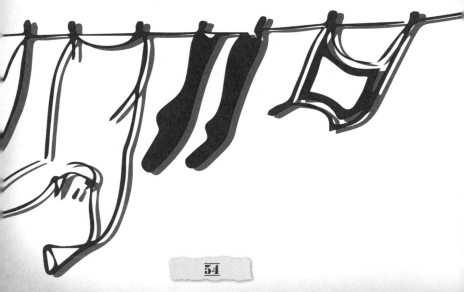

THE
SANCHEZ SISTERS

Lola Sanchez was angry. Her town had been invaded by Union soldiers, her father was wrongly accused of spying and imprisoned, and now the Union soldiers had moved into the Sanchez home in Palatka, FL. Lola and her sisters, Francesca (nicknamed "Panchita") and Eugenia, decided it was time they took revenge. They decided to spy on the Union invaders.

The girls started their spy work by inviting the Union soldiers to evenings of dinner and conversation. The soldiers enjoyed visiting the pretty Sanchez sisters and soon they were bringing guests with them. Some of these guests were high-ranking officers of the Union Army. The soldiers thought the Sanchez sisters were lovely and harmless, so they talked freely about battle plans and troop movements.

On the evening of May 21, 1862, Union soldiers were enjoying a supper served by the Sanchez sisters. The soldiers began discussing a raid that was planned for the next morning. Lola listened closely. She knew this was critical information and she needed to warn the Confederate commander.

Lola consulted with her sisters, and they formed a plan: Panchita and Eugenia would entertain the soldiers and serve supper while Lola took a horse and headed for the Confederate camp. The girls all knew it was a huge risk. It was at least a mile and a half to the camp, with a river to cross. If the soldiers suspected that Lola was missing, there would be questions they could not answer. They might end up in prison with their father, but they decided it was worth the risk.

Lola headed off into the night. She knew that once she reached the end of the forest, she would have to find a way to cross the river to reach the Confederate camp. Luck was with Lola and the ferry was running that night. She convinced the ferryman to watch her horse as she rode the ferry across the river. Once the ferry docked, Lola hiked up her long skirts and ran for the camp. She stopped the first guard she met. He listened but could not leave his post, so he gave Lola his horse and she rode the rest of the way to find Captain Dickison.

As soon as she had told her story and knew that Captain Dickison believed her, Lola mounted the horse and rode back to the Confederate guard. She returned his horse and ran for the ferry. She made it back home on her own horse in just an hour and a half. She smoothed her clothes and went in to laugh and talk with the soldiers as if nothing had ever happened.

That night, Captain Dickison and his soldiers crossed the river and set a trap for the Union gunboat. The Union soldiers never knew what happened. The USS Columbine was set on fire and the Union soldiers were captured. The Sanchez sisters were never suspected and continued their spy work until the end of the war.

After the war, all three of the Sanchez sisters married former Confederate soldiers. Lola died in 1895, but Panchita lived until 1931 and Eugenia until 1932. In 1909, their spy service was recognized and they were honored with their names engraved on a plaque of Confederate heroines.

SECRET MESSAGES

In a war, information is gold. If you are able to learn your enemies' plans, you can stop an attack and save lives. Of course, the same is true for both sides. Everyone wants to know what the other side is planning. That's why secret codes are so valuable. If your side has a way to send message that no one else understands, you have the advantage.

Both the Union and Confederate armies used a variety of codes. Some of them were more successful than others. The Stager Cipher was the most important code for the Union. It was never broken by the Confederacy and was used to transmit telegrams.

Immediately after the Civil War started, the governor of Ohio hired Anson Stager to invent a code that could be used on the telegraph. The governor knew it was critical that information sent on the telegraph be coded. The messages went through several offices before they reached their final destination. In each office, there was an operator writing down the information and then transmitting it onto the next telegraph line. It would be simple to plant a spy in a telegraph office and then the enemy would know everything that was planned.

Anson Stager took his job seriously and designed an amazingly intricate code that required an entire book to interpret it! The code became known as the Stager Cipher and it was so effective that it was adopted by the Union War Department as its official telegraph code.

To protect against the code falling into enemy hands, Stager issued an order that no one besides the official telegraph operators could see the codebook. When Stager said no one, he meant it—even President Lincoln was not allowed to look at the codebook! The Stager Cipher was used for the entire war and was never cracked.

The pigpen cipher was much less secure than the Stager Cipher, but it was still used for some low-level communication. Soldiers would pass notes to each other using the pigpen cipher. It was a cipher that had been used by a civic organization called the Free Masons. Many business men belonged to the Free Masons so they knew the code and used it during the war. It was a simple alphabet substitution that used a grid system to replace letters. The common variety of the code looked like this:

WANTED:
CODEBREAKERS

The Confederacy got so desperate
to crack the Stager Cipher that
they published Union messages
in Southern newspapers asking
the public to help break the code.
No one ever did.

A sample message would look like this:

Regular alphabet: *Help is on the way*

Pigpen alphabet: ⅃L⌐⊓ ⊡∨ ⊓⅂ ∀⅃L ＜⅃∧

It was easy to memorize and simple to use, but it was also easy to crack the code. It wasn't a great code for top secret information.

Spies often used cipher wheels to exchange messages. To send and read the code, each person had to have a cipher wheel. By turning the wheel, the sender selected which code was going to be used. The code was written down and the receiver had to dial his or her cipher wheel to the same setting. Then, the message could be decoded. Cipher wheels have been used since the mid-1400s and were used by the Vatican to send coded messages.

HOW TO WRECK A
RAILROAD

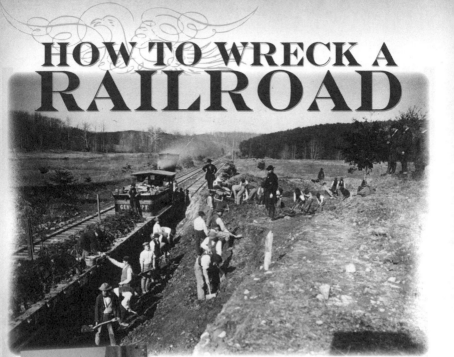

The railroad tracks had been pried out of the ground and bent at right angles. It was a mess, and it wasn't the first time it had happened. Trains had to be halted until the track could be replaced because Confederate soldiers were destroying the tracks. Union Brigadier General Herman Haupt was disgusted, and he was not going to put up with it anymore. He was ready for revenge and retaliation.

Haupt was a trained railroad engineer, and he used his knowledge to devise his own methods of wrecking a railroad. He then published an instruction manual for Union Calvary men that showed them the best ways to wreck tracks behind Confederate lines.

The manual stressed speed. Haupt advised soldiers to use hit and run tactics in enemy territory and he advised against carrying crowbars. They were too heavy. Instead he supplied Union saboteurs with small iron wedges that could be pounded with axes to quickly pry up the rails. Using the methods in his manual, Haupt bragged that four men could remove a rail in 3 minutes.

Even more effective than wrecking the rails was to wreck a bridge. Haupt came up with a special 8-inch-long "torpedo" (bomb) that consisted of metal cylinders filled with explosive powder and equipped with a fuse. The soldier was instructed to drill a hole in the main brace and insert the torpedo. It was so effective that just two torpedoes could take out a simple truss bridge. Larger bridges just needed more torpedoes.

Another useful invention was a special steel hook. It looked like a giant horseshoe, but when a long handle was place in the top of the hook, it would act as a pry bar. By applying pressure to the pry bar, the hook would rip the train rail from its track and twist the steel bar. This was especially damaging because twisted steel had to be sent back to the forge to be repaired.

As effective as Haupt's tactics were at destroying railroads, he was even better at fixing them. He organized a war construction corps that had nearly 10,000 men, many of whom were former slaves who volunteered for the job. The men were an unstoppable workforce who relaid hundreds of miles of tracks destroyed by Confederate raiders and reconstructed dozens of bridges in just a few weeks' time.

In 1864, the Confederates destroyed a 780-foot bridge over the Chattahoochee River in Georgia. It took Haupt's men less than 5 days to reconstruct the bridge. When the Confederates destroyed 35 miles of track in Georgia that same year, they were sure they had put a stop to Union rail shipments. But Haupt's men had the railroad back to full operation in just 13 days. Herman Haupt had his revenge and never let the Confederates stop his trains from running.

Make a Cipher Wheel

SPY TRAINING

Spies in the Civil War often used cipher wheels to make and interpret coded messages. The wheel tells you which letter to substitute to make the code. If you give your spy partner a copy of the cipher wheel, he or she can use it to read the coded message you have sent.

First you will need to make two copies of each of the cipher wheels below—one of each for you and one of each for your spy partner.

Materials:
- ❑ Copies of the cipher wheel templates
- ❑ Scissors
- ❑ Brad or safety pin

Cut out both wheels. Place the smaller wheel inside the larger wheel and attach them with a paper brad or a safety pin. This is the cipher wheel.

First write this practice message: I am a super spy.

Spin the wheel so that the inside letter/number wheel lines up with the outside letters. For this trial run, you need to line up the wheel so that the outside A is aligned with inside D3. This will be the cipher coder you will use to write your message. Whenever you make a code with the cipher wheel, you must write down what code you are using. For example, if you move the inside wheel so that A lines up with E4, it will be a different code.

Using the code D3, you will substitute the letters in your message for the letters on the cipher wheel.

Your code will look like this:

I	A M	A	S U P E R	S P Y
Q	I U	I	A C X M Z	A X G

To make a new code, just move the cipher wheel. The next step is to make your own message and see if your friend can decipher the code. Be sure to tell him or her which code you are using!

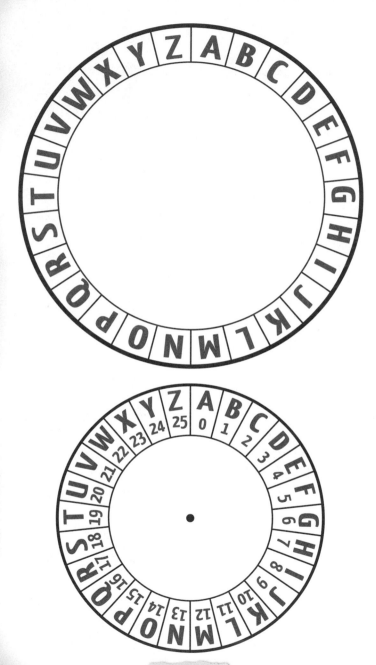

SPY TRAINING

Make a Scytale

A scytale is an ancient way of sending secret messages. It uses two dowel rods of the same size and a long strip of paper. The strip of paper is wrapped around the sender's dowel rod and the message is written while the paper is wrapped around the rod. When you unwrap the paper, it looks like a list of letters. When the receiver gets the message, she wraps it around her dowel rot and she can read the message. The secret is having dowel rods that are the same size. Otherwise it's pretty hard to read the message!

Materials:

❑ Two dowel rods of the exact same circumference and length

❑ A long strip of paper about 1/2-inch wide

❑ Marker or pencil

❑ Spy friend

First wrap the strip of paper around the dowel rod (scytale). Write the message you wish to send. Then unwrap the strip of paper. Give it to your friend and tell her to wrap the paper around her scytale (dowel rod) and have her read the message.

SPECIAL
WEAPONS

ABRAHAM LINCOLN'S SECRET WEAPON

Lincoln and his army needed information. How could he find out what the secret plans of the Confederacy were? How could he win the war and keep the United States together? Secretary of War Edwin Stanton had an idea: They should secretly take control of the telegraph lines.

MILLIONS OF MESSAGES

During the Civil War, Union officers and officials sent 6.5 million telegrams. That was an average of 4,500 messages per day. This is why cutting the telegraph lines was such a problem and a strategy of war—if you cut the lines, communication stopped.

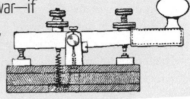

The telegraph was invented in 1830s, and by the time of the Civil War, it was in common use. Telegraph lines had been strung across the country from New York to California. For about $1, anyone could send a short message across the country. Families often received information about births and deaths by telegraph, and business people sent important messages from one city to another. In the days before telephones, the telegraph was the primary form of fast, long-distance communication. A letter could take several days or even weeks to get from one part of the country to another. A telegraph would be delivered the same day it was sent.

Secretary of War Stanton realized that Confederate and Union officers were sending vast amounts of information across the telegraph lines. Information about troop movements or shipments could be coded, but those codes could also be broken. All they had to do was reroute the telegraph lines to go through the war office. This way, Stanton and his office could keep tabs on any and all information sent across the telegraph lines.

It may have seemed like a vast invasion of privacy, but Lincoln believed that it was important to the security of the nation to obtain as much knowledge as he could. He approved Stanton's plan and for the duration of the war, all telegraph communications went through Stanton's office before going out to their intended recipient.

Stanton and his office had to sort through hundreds of messages. Many of them were family or business communications, but there was also information from Confederate generals, information of arms shipments, reports from Confederate field officers, and calls for assistance. Lincoln became a regular visitor to the war office, dropping by nearly every afternoon to see what Stanton's men had discovered.

With the aid of the telegraph information, Lincoln and the Union generals were able to make battle plans that eventually helped the North win the war. And it was all because of Lincoln's secret weapon, the telegraph.

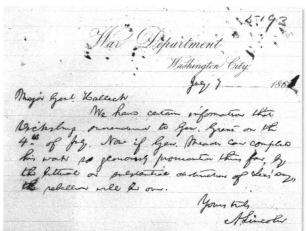

July 7, 1863, three days after the Battle of Gettysburg and the fall of Vicksburg, President Abraham Lincoln penned this note to his General-in-Chief Henry Halleck. After General Halleck received the note from the President, he quoted the information verbatim in a telegram to General Meade on the same day.

HARMONICA PISTOL

What looks like a musical instrument but packs the wallop of a revolver? A harmonica pistol, of course.

The harmonica pistol was an inventor's solution to building a multishot gun. The first guns that were capable of firing more than one round without reloading were made in the 1500s and were called pepperbox revolvers. These guns had three or more barrels and this caused the gun to be very front heavy and difficult to aim.

The harmonica gun was lighter because it had one barrel and the shot was loaded into a steel slide. The slide could be loaded with 9 or 10 shots, which was three or four more than a traditional revolver. Problem was, it took more time to load than a revolver. Plus, with the slide hanging off to one side of the gun, it was more difficult to have accurate aim. But the reason most soldiers probably disliked the harmonica pistol was that the metal slide made it impossible to store in a holster. A revolver may have only had six shots, but the soldier could pull it out and be ready at a moment's notice. The harmonica pistol was used in the Civil War, but it probably looked better than it shot.

WINANS STEAM GUN

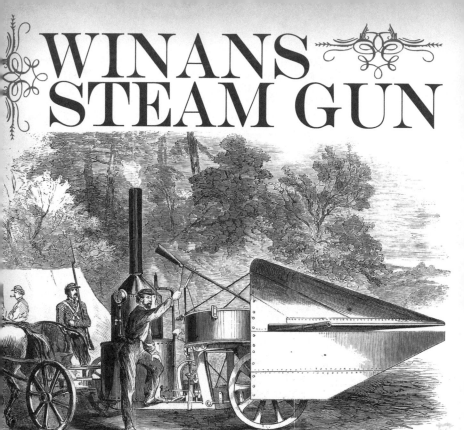

They claimed it could fire 200 shots a minute.

The giant gun was nearly the size of a fire engine and had a giant conical metal shield that made it look like a metal monster. Built by Ohio inventors William Joslin and Charles Dickinson, this massive automatic weapon sat on an armored train carriage and used steam to fire projectiles.

Dickinson tried to sell the gun to the city of Baltimore, but in the corrupt city, police took the weapon from Dickinson. They planned to use it on Union recruits as they traveled through Baltimore. Riots broke out in Baltimore, and the gun was never fired, but it was damaged. After things calmed down a bit, the gun was returned to Dickinson and repaired at the city's expense.

Still looking for a buyer for his super steam gun, Dickinson decided to take the gun to Harper's Ferry to try to sell it to the Confederates. The Union didn't like the idea of the Confederates having an all-powerful steam gun, so they stole it. The steam gun spent the rest of the war on display, but it never actually saw battle.

People have always wondered how powerful the gun really was. Could it really shoot 200 rounds a minute? Was it a weapon of huge destruction? Modern-day investigators have built reproductions of the steam gun and the results have been mixed. Tests by both students at MIT (Massachusetts Institute of Technology) and the TV show *Mythbusters* demonstrated that the gun is capable of firing but not at the projected rate of 200 rounds per minute. In reality, the Winans Steam Gun looked like a super weapon but was less reliable than a regular powder fire gun.

Civil War Myth
BUSTED
See how the *Mythbusters* crew tested the Winans Steam Gun in this clip from the show:
https://www.youtube.com/watch?v=YKhLgPyymfU

SECRET
SUBMARINE

H.L. Hunley was a wealthy Southern lawyer who was dedicated to creating a secret weapon to help the Confederacy win the war. He wanted to build a boat

that could not be seen by other ships
. . . a boat that could deliver a deadly
torpedo that the enemy would never
expect. He wanted to build a submarine.

With the help of two New Orleans machine shop operators, Hunley designed and built a three-man submarine called the *Pioneer*. Unfortunately, just as the ship was finished, the Union Army invaded New Orleans. Hunley and his crew did not want the Union to learn about their secret weapon so they scuttled (sank) the *Pioneer* so the Union could not capture it.

Hunley and his team moved to Mobile, AL, and continued working on an underwater vessel. They completed a larger submarine but it sank in rough waters before it could even be tested. Hunley was not ready to give up.

A third ship was built. This one was much larger. Cylinder-shaped and 30 feet long, this boat was named the *H. L. Hunley* after its inventor. The submarine was only 4 feet wide and 5 feet high and was supposed to carry a crew of nine men. It was a very tight squeeze.

The submarine was outfitted with a long bench, where eight of the crew members were supposed to sit side by side and operate a hand crank propeller. The ninth man steered the submarine and operated the ballast. When the ballast tank was filled with water, it would cause the submarine to submerge. When the water was let out and replaced by air, the submarine would surface.

The nose of the Hunley submarine had a 22-foot-long pine pole or boom attached. At the end of the pole was a torpedo. The submarine would attack by ramming the torpedo into the side of the enemy ship. The submarine would then sail away and the torpedo would be detonated from a safe distance using a line attached to a trigger. In theory, it should have worked.

The Hunley submarine made a successful trial run at Mobile before it was loaded onto a train and shipped to Charleston, SC. The plan was to use the submarine to attack Northern ships and break the blockade that was stopping shipments of goods and medicine to the South.

SINKING SHIP

The Union also built a submarine called the *Alligator*. It was designed by French inventor Brutus de Villeroi. He had invented a chemical device to fill the submarine with fresh air, but before it could be tested, Villeroi got in a fight with the Navy contractor and took his plans back to France. The submarine built without his plans was tested, but lost at sea. The Union never built another submarine.

A volunteer crew was organized to man the submarine. They practiced in the harbor and got the submarine to successfully submerge, travel across the harbor, and return to the surface. All was going well, until one day, the vessel flooded and sank, killing five of the crewmen. The ship was raised and repaired, and another volunteer crew got ready to test the machine.

Determined that his secret weapon was the solution to the Union blockade, Hunley himself volunteered for the next trial. This time the submarine sank and killed all of the sailors, including Hunley.

Amazingly, another crew of Confederate sailors volunteered to take on a mission in the submarine. This time, there were no trials. They were to attack the Union blockade. Their goal was to sink the Union *Housatonic*, a 23-gun sloop of war.

The crew left port at 8 p.m. on February 17, 1864. In the dark of the winter night, the Union soldiers saw something underwater headed toward their ship. Some of the sailors thought it might be a large fish or porpoise, but a few minutes later, a huge explosion rocked the *Housatonic* and the wooden ship sank.

On the other side of the harbor, the Confederate sailors waited for the Hunley submarine to reappear. It never returned. The ship had sunk again, killing every man on board. This time, the submarine stayed submerged until 2000, when divers discovered the hull of the 136-year-old submarine. The *Hunley* was raised and is now on display at a museum in South Carolina. The *Hunley* holds the distinction of being the first combat submarine to successfully sink a war ship.

THE DEVIL'S
COFFEE MILL

Abraham Lincoln was a hard-nosed lawyer and a skeptical Midwesterner. He was not easily impressed, but when Wilson Agar demonstrated his new invention, Lincoln was astonished. Using a hand crank that looked somewhat like a coffee mill, Agar's gun could fire an amazing 120 rounds of ammunition per minute. Lincoln had never seen anything like it; neither had most of the world.

At the start of the Civil War, the most common gun was a muzzle-loaded rifle musket. A well-trained soldier could reload his gun every 15–30 seconds. The most he could shoot in one minute was four rounds of ammunition. The Agar gun must have looked like something out of the future. Other observers commented that if the gun looked like a coffee mill grinder, then it must make a Devil's brew. Lincoln was so impressed that he ordered 10 of the guns for the Union and paid an astonishing $1,300 for each gun. (In today's money that would be approximately $35,000 per gun!)

The first guns were shipped to the 28th Pennsylvania regiment. After testing out the gun, First Sergeant Ambrose Henry Hayward wrote home to his sister and said: "We have got two Union Guns that were presented to the 28th. They are fired by turning a crank . . . I cannot describe it but when the men saw it first they thought it was a sausage grinder."

The rapid shooting that so amazed President Lincoln and the soldiers was also the greatest problem with the gun. The rapid fire caused the barrel of the gun to overheat. Soldiers had to let the barrel cool between shootings or switch in a different barrel. In addition, officials believed the gun used up too much ammunition to be practical. The guns actually saw very little use in battle and were eventually only used to guard bridges and railroad overpasses.

Still, the Civil War was the first war to see the use of machine guns. Innovations and modifications during the next several years led to the invention of the modern rapid fire machine gun.

Better Than Any Gun

Believe it or not, during the Civil War, a good map was a secret weapon. In 1861, there were very few accurate maps because most Americans never traveled far from home. When the war started, many military units got lost on their way to battle. It turned out that a good mapmaker was a better secret weapon than any gun!

SPY BALLOONS

Thaddeus Lowe, ca. 1890

Every general in the Civil War dreamed of a secret weapon that could tell what his enemy had planned. If only there were some way to get a bird's eye view of the land around the troops. Then, the generals could see where their enemy was headed. But in 1861, there were no airplanes. It would be 42 years before the Wright brothers would experiment at Kitty Hawk. It would be more than 100 years before astronauts would visit the moon or scientists would launch satellites. In 1861, there was only one way to get a spy in the air and that was with a balloon.

Thaddeus S. C. Lowe was just the man for the job. He had been interested in flight since he was a boy, when he sent his cat sailing in a basket attached to a kite. During the 1850s, he began performing outdoors as an aeronaut and had become one of the best in the country. With more than 10 years of experience, Lowe was the perfect man to be put in charge of the Union's aerial reconnaissance.

The 29-year-old Lowe began monitoring troop movements from his balloon in November of 1861. Lowe and his crew converted an abandoned coal barge into a floating platform that Lowe used as a launch pad for his balloon. It could also be used to carry the balloon from one launch site to another, so it was, in fact, America's first aircraft carrier.

Typically, Lowe would make his flights in the early morning, sometimes soaring as high as 1,000 feet. He was able to view the movements of Confederate troops, spot the locations of cannons, and locate campgrounds.

The Confederates hated Lowe and his balloon. They often tried to shoot him down, but the cannons and rifles of the day did not have enough firepower to reach the balloon. Lowe's balloon was not in real danger but his launch crew had to watch out for sniper fire.

Unable to shoot him down, the Confederates worked to fool Lowe by giving him incorrect information. They would paint logs black and set them out to look like cannons. They also camped under the cover of trees so he could not see all of their tents and get an accurate troop count.

Lowe worked for the Union as an observer until May of 1863. He resigned after his superiors reduced his pay and returned to private business. Lowe loved flying and kept inventing until his death in 1913 at the age of 71. When he died, he was working on designs for his own airplane.

You can experiment with making your own mini hot air balloon on p. 93!

INTREPID

GERM WARFARE

Germ warfare is something only found in science fiction movies, when evil warlords unleash a deadly disease to wipe out their enemy. That's just the stuff of stories, right? Wrong!

During the Civil War, there were several plots to use germ warfare to affect the enemy. Fortunately, none of them actually worked. The science behind germs was still in its formative stages. Scientists understood that germs caused some disease but did not know always know how the germs were transmitted.

It was rumored that some Confederate soldiers took the clothes of people infected with smallpox and sent them in trunks to the North in the hopes that it would cause an outbreak of the disease. Another scheme was organized by Confederate doctor Luke Pryor Blackburn. He was a physician from Kentucky who had worked extensively treating epidemics of yellow fever.

During Civil War times, yellow fever outbreaks happened every year during the warm season. Sometimes the outbreaks were small, but other times there were hundreds of people infected with numerous deaths. Doctors were not sure how to stop the outbreaks, but they thought there was some sort of "germ" that infected the people.

You can view a video about the plans for biological warfare during the Civil War here:
http://www.history.com/topics/american-civil-war/american-civil-war-history/videos/
civil-war-biological-warfare.

Dr. Blackburn thought that he could use yellow fever as a weapon against the North. In the spring of 1864, there was a severe yellow fever epidemic in Bermuda. Dr. Blackburn volunteered his service to help the sick and dying, but the philanthropic doctor had ulterior motives. As he was helping the people, he collected the bedding and clothes of the people who died. He packed them in trunks and had them shipped to the North. He believed that the clothes and bedding would be distributed to needy people and the yellow fever germs would cause an epidemic of yellow fever in the Union states.

A man who was supposed to be helping Dr. Blackburn with the project, Godfrey Hyams, had a change of heart. He reported Dr. Blackburn to Union authorities, and Dr. Blackburn was later arrested.

Nearly 40 years later, Army surgeon Dr. Walter Reed proved that yellow fever, now called malaria, could not be transmitted through clothing or bodily fluids from a sick person. The only way a person could be infected with yellow fever is through the bite of a mosquito. Dr. Blackburn's plan for germ warfare would have never worked.

SPECIAL DELIVERY
FOR THE PRESIDENT

One of the trunks packed with garments supposedly contaminated with yellow fever was meant to be delivered to the White House—the story goes that Hyams, Blackburn's accomplice, was told to deliver it to Lincoln and say it was from an anonymous admirer! Although Hyams changed his mind, President Lincoln would be assassinated 2 days after he reported Blackburn to the authorities.

IRONCLADS
THE SECRET WEAPON
OF THE NAVY

It was a calm afternoon in March of 1862. Sailors' laundry waved from the riggings of five Union warships. They had been blockading the James River for days with no real fighting, so the sailors had washed their clothes and hung them out to dry.

Then, in the distance, the sailors saw a strange-looking boat slowly moving toward them.

"All hands on deck!"

Sailors ran to their stations and peered down the river at what looked like a floating barn, or as one sailor described it, "a huge half submerged crocodile." They had never seen anything like it, and it was definitely a Confederate ship.

As soon as the ship came into range, the Union warships fired on the floating barn, but the cannonballs bounced off the Confederate ship like rubber balls. The Confederate ship rammed the Union ship *Cumberland* and sank her. Then it blasted apart another Union ship with its guns and ran a third ship aground. The Union sailors were terrified. What was this terrible secret weapon the Confederates had created?

It was the CSS *Virginia*, one of the first ironclad ships built in America. Ironclads were not new. The first iron-covered ship was launched by the French Navy in 1859. The ships were steam-powered gunboats covered in iron. The Confederates decided to build their own version of an ironclad, took the salvaged hull of the captured USS *Merrimack*, and covered the ship with 4 inches of iron plating. It was 275 feet long, carried 10 guns (cannons), and had a deadly 4-foot-long iron battering ram. The metal protected the ship from cannonballs and turned the ship into a floating fortress.

At the end of the day, *Virginia* had destroyed three of the blockade ships and sent two others running for cover. The *Virginia* and its crew pulled back at night with plans to return in the daylight to finish the fight.

The next day, the Union soldiers had a surprise waiting for the Confederates: They had called in their own ironclad ship, the USS *Monitor*. This ship was smaller than the *Virginia* and instead of looking like a floating barn, it looked more like a mud turtle—flat on the bottom and rounded in the middle with a revolving gun turret and two 11-inch guns.

The ships did battle for nearly 4 hours. The cannonballs rained off of the sides of both ships. Frustrated sailors tried using hand guns to shoot in the portals. In the end, it was considered a draw and both ships backed off.

It was the first time the world had ever seen two ironclad ships fight, and it changed naval warfare forever. It became apparent to all that the ironclad ship was far superior to

Line engraving published in *Harper's Weekly*, 1863, depicting USS *Monitor* sinking in a storm off Cape Hatteras on the night of December 30–31, 1862; a boat is taking off crewmen, and USS *Rhode Island* is in the background

wooden vessels and all ships in subsequent wars were made of metal.

As tough as the ironclads were against the wooden ships, they were not invincible. Neither the *Monitor* nor the *Virginia* survived the year. The Confederates had to blow up the *Virginia* to prevent the Union from capturing it. The *Monitor* sank in a storm off the Outer Banks of North Carolina on New Year's Eve 1862.

IN THE LIMELIGHT

Darkness was a real tool of the Civil War. Electric lights did not come into common use until 20 years after the war ended. Homes and buildings were illuminated by candles or kerosene lanterns. In large cities, there were gaslight lamps, but the countryside was very dark at night.

The darkness was seen as an advantage for raiders on both sides of the war. Under cover of deep darkness, raiders could sneak into camps unseen. Prisoners could escape because there were no search lights. And battle usually ceased at night-fall, because neither side could see where it was shooting.

Inventor Robert Grant believed that light could be used as a secret weapon. By using his creation, calcium light, the Union could blind and attack the Confederate troops. Calcium light was created by heating up calcium oxide (commonly called lime). Under intense heat, the lime would create a bright white light. These lights were used in theatres before electric lights were invented. This is where the saying "in the limelight" originated.

The problem with calcium lights was that sometimes the intense heat would cause fires. It was not safe enough for use in homes, but Robert Grant believed it could be very effective on the battlefield. He offered his services to Union General Benjamin F. Butler.

General Butler allowed Robert Grant to install his calcium lights on the parapets at Fort Monroe. The bright light scared off would-be saboteurs and made it impossible for enemy ships to slip through in the dark. The experiment was deemed a success, and Robert Grant proposed forming a special army unit called the Calcium Light Regiment. His ideas was that this special unit would do its fighting at night. The soldiers would carry calcium lights and use the lights to illuminate their path and, at the same time, blind their enemies. Permission was given for Robert Grant to form the Calcium Light Sharpshooters, but the troop was never put into action.

Calcium lights were used in in July of 1863 during a Union siege of Fort Wagner in South Carolina. The Confederates were holding the fort, and the Union could not route them. General Quincy Adams Gilmore called on Robert Grant to cover the fort with two calcium lights. The lights were set up about 750 yards away from Fort Wagner. A makeshift laboratory was put together near the Union trenches and was staffed by 20 soldiers and 20 civilians. They made the necessary hydrogen and oxygen gasses right on the battle field.

With the aid of reflectors, Robert Grant focused his calcium lights on the fort and left the Union trenches in the dark.

Under the intense light, it was impossible for the Confederates to come out at night and make any repairs to the fort. The light blinded the Confederates so they could not aim their guns correctly, and it kept them from sleeping. After a few weeks, the Confederates abandoned the fort and the Union took over. The calcium light siege was deemed a success.

After the war, calcium lights were used for slideshows, parades, and nighttime sporting events, but they were soon forgotten with the invention of Edison's electric lightbulb.

QUAKER GUNS

"Quaker guns" (named for the pacifist religious group) were fake artillery used by both sides during the Civil War. The

fake guns helped the army look bigger and better armed than it really was. Often, these were just logs painted black to look like cannons!

SPY TRAINING

Secret Map

Maps were incredibly important during the Civil War. Printed maps were expensive and most people did not own any maps. In addition, parts of the South and West did not have detailed maps, so any map was considered valuable. Often spies were sent out to make maps of local areas to help officers know where they needed to send their troops.

You can practice your spy skills by making a map of your own neighborhood.

Materials:
- ❏ Paper
- ❏ Pencil
- ❏ Some detective work!
- ❏ A test subject (friend)

First make a legend for your map. A legend is a key to what each symbol represents. For example, a dotted line might mean a sidewalk. A thick heavy line might mean a road.

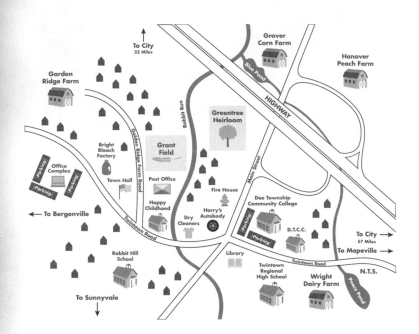

Learn which directions are north, south, east, and west. Write the directions on your map. Then, draw in all of the details of your neighborhood. Put houses, businesses, trees, and anything that is a landmark or a place you need to remember.

When your map is finished, check to see if it works. Hide a small token somewhere in your neighborhood, then give the map to a friend and put an X where you have hidden the item. See if your friend can find it. If he or she can find it quickly, you have created an excellent map!

SPY TRAINING

Hot Air Balloon

Hot air balloons aren't difficult to make. They just require an airtight balloon and a source of hot air. You can demonstrate how a hot air balloon works with this simple experiment. You will need an adult to help do this experiment because it involves a stove and some really hot water!

Materials:

- ❏ Glass bottle with narrow mouth
- ❏ Balloon
- ❏ Stove
- ❏ Tongs or oven mitts
- ❏ Pot half full of water

Place the uninflated balloon over the mouth of the glass bottle. Have an adult boil the water in the pot. When the water is boiling, have an adult use the tongs or mitts to set the bottle in the boiling water. Wait a few moments and see what happens to the balloon.

As air gets hot, it expands and will inflate the balloon. Hot air is lighter than cold air, so a balloon that is filled with hot air will float. And that's how some of the Civil War balloons worked!

If you can't do this experiment at home, you might enjoy watching a video of this phenomenon in action! See https://www.youtube.com/ watch?v=2McLEs_iQhw for a video showing how this experiment works.

SECRET FORCES

JOHNNY CLEM, BOY SOLDIER

Sgt. John Clem, 1867

Twelve-year-old Johnny Clem knew the dispatch he was carrying was important. Union Major General George H. Thomas was counting on Clem to get the message to his troops. Shots whistled around Clem, and he urged his horse to go faster. But the horse stumbled and fell—it had been hit by a Confederate bullet. Clem scrambled to his feet. He couldn't help his horse, and the longer he stayed on the battlefield, the more likely it was that Clem himself would be shot. He did what he knew he had to do and ran to the front to deliver his message.

This wasn't the first time Clem had found himself in the middle of a battle. At the start of the war in 1861, 9-year-old Clem ran away from home and joined the 22nd Michigan

Regiment as its drummer boy. Clem actually fought in the Battle of Chickamauga. His drum had been shot and destroyed, but his fellow soldiers gave him a musket that was cut down to his size. He used it to defend himself against an attacking Confederate soldier.

By the time Clem was 12, he had been promoted to Lance Sergeant. At one point, he was captured and held as a prisoner of war, but was released after a few weeks in a prisoner exchange. Clem was wounded twice and was discharged from the army in 1864 at the end of the war. He was 13 years old.

Six years later, a 19-year-old John Clem appealed to President Ulysses S. Grant to return to the military he loved. Grant commissioned him as a second lieutenant in the army. Clem served in the army until 1916, when he retired at the age of 64 with the rank of Major General. He was the last Civil War veteran to serve in the army. He lived to the ripe old age of 85.

BOY SOLDIERS

Johnny Clem may have been one of the youngest boys to serve in the Civil War but he was not the only young soldier on the battlefield. It is estimated that 300 Civil War soldiers were age 13 or under. Most of them served as drummers, fife players, or message carriers.

THE
GRAY GHOST

John Singleton Mosby was a small man. He had been sickly as a child and was often picked on by bullies. His response to being teased and harassed was to learn to defend himself. Mosby became a scrappy fighter, an excellent horseman, and a quick thinker.

It all served him well when the Civil War broke out. A native of Virginia, Mosby was a Southerner, but he was against the idea of secession. He wanted the Southern states to stay in the Union and work out their differences. Still, when the war was declared, Mosby joined the Confederate Army. He became a member of J. E. B. Stuart's Cavalry Scouts and his horsemanship skills were quickly noticed.

Stuart selected Mosby to be in charge of a special group of rangers. Mosby had his pick of men and he selected two dozen exceptional horsemen. Their assignment was to conduct raids on the Union, destroy equipment, and cause as many problems as possible for the North.

Mosby trained his men to be experts in stealth. They learned to move quietly through the woods and to hide in the shadows. They would wait patiently until the timing was perfect, then swoop in and attack their target. The Union soldiers claimed Mosby and his men would appear as quietly as a ghost. The Union soldiers started calling him the Gray Ghost and they feared raids by Mosby and his "guerilla army."

Brigadier General Edwin Stoughton was stationed in the Manassas, VA, area. It was part of the country patrolled by the Gray Ghost and his guerrillas. Mosby and his men had captured soldiers and ammunition, destroyed guns and equipment, and stolen Union horses. Edwin Stoughton wanted Mosby caught and put in prison.

On March 7, 1862, Stoughton was sound asleep when he felt someone slap him on the rear. He woke up to see a small man standing in the dark room. He sat up and yelled at the man, asking what he was doing.

The man asked, "Do you know Mosby?"

Stoughton was relieved for a moment. "Yes," he replied. "You've caught him?"

"No," the man said. "But he has caught you!"

That night, Mosby and his rangers captured 30 soldiers, two captains, one general, and 58 horses without ever firing a gun. When Abraham Lincoln heard about Mosby's raid, he remarked that he did not mind losing a general: "I can make a much better brigadier in five minutes, but the horses cost a hundred and twenty-five dollars apiece."

Mosby's Rangers were so successful that the area they patrolled became known as "Mosby's Confederacy." He and his men kept complete control of the land lying between the Blue Ridge and Bull Run Mountains.

After the war, Mosby joined the Republican Party, which was the same party that Abraham Lincoln belonged to. It made many Southerners angry, because they felt Mosby was acting like a traitor to the South. Mosby became good friends with Ulysses S. Grant and even became his campaign manager and helped him win the presidency. Eventually, Mosby served his country in many capacities including as the U.S. Consul in Hong Kong. He died in 1916 at the age of 82.

As he reflected back on his days in the Civil War, he wrote, "It is a classical maxim that it is sweet and becoming to die for one's country; but whoever has seen the horrors of a battlefield feels that it is far sweeter to live for it."

Recycled Weapons?

With supplies and munitions in short supply in the Confederacy, General Josiah Gorgas was tasked with the difficult job of organizing the production of weapons for the South. He 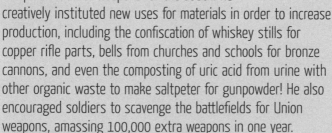 creatively instituted new uses for materials in order to increase production, including the confiscation of whiskey stills for copper rifle parts, bells from churches and schools for bronze cannons, and even the composting of uric acid from urine with other organic waste to make saltpeter for gunpowder! He also encouraged soldiers to scavenge the battlefields for Union weapons, amassing 100,000 extra weapons in one year.

THE JESSIE SCOUTS

It was the most dangerous of all disguises: the Confederate uniform. If a Union trooper was caught pretending to be a Confederate soldier, he would be killed. But it was also the perfect disguise. Dressed in a Confederate uniform, a scout could travel behind enemy lines and go places a civilian would never be allowed. It was a risk the men of the Jessie Scouts volunteered to take—and many of them paid with their lives.

Arch Rowand was one Jessie Scout who survived the war and lived to be an old man. In an interview with *Harper's Monthly* magazine, Rowand explained that the Jessie Scouts were all volunteers and they knew the risks of spying in the enemy's uniform. But they also witnessed the confusion it caused for the Confederate Army. They became suspicious of even their own men and, not knowing who to trust, they trusted no one. At night, they were just as likely to shoot at a man in a gray uniform as one in blue.

One assignment Rowand was given was to deliver an important message from General Sheridan to General Grant. Rowand and his partner were given two fast horses and ordered to get through the rebel lines as fast as they could. If they were caught, they were to eat the dispatches (the notes) from Sheridan.

The two men rode 145 miles and made it to General Grant's camp the next day. The entire camp was surprised when two Confederate soldiers rode in asking for the General. But that wasn't the last surprise for Grant: As Sheridan's troops marched to join Grant, more men in Confederate uniforms began to appear in camp. Most of them arrived with Confederate prisoners in tow. Some of them hauled in captured weapons, and all of them brought information.

By the end of the war, the Jessie Scouts were experts at spying. They expanded their disguises to include the civilian clothes of farmers and businessmen, but their most successful schemes involved dressing as enemy officers and delivering false information.

Arch Rowand continued his work with the Jessie Scouts after the end of the Civil War. General Sheridan selected several of the scouts to go with him through Texas and into Mexico on a spying mission for the United States. There they collected vital information on the activities of the French, Austrian, and Mexican Imperial troops who had been supporting the Confederacy.

The Jessie Scouts learned the craft of spying and their successful work helped pave the way for the modern arm of the United States Secret Service.

ANOTHER KIND OF DISGUISE

Amy Clarke joined her husband in the fight during the Civil War, disguising herself as "Richard Anderson" to join a Tennessee unit of the Confederacy. Although her husband died at Shiloh, she continued to fight until she was wounded and captured by Union soldiers. When they discovered she was a woman, she was sent back to the South wearing a dress.

McNEILL'S RANGERS

John Harrison McNeill

Their target was the B&O railroad. Their assignment—to stop Union troop movements any way they could.

Captain John Harrison McNeill was put in charge of 210 men and given the near impossible task of patrolling more than 100 miles of the Allegheny Mountains in West Virginia. This meant that his troops were often split up into small patrol bands and used a hit and run method. They would charge into Union camps and confiscate weapons and food, or they would raid Union-held towns and try to cause problems by burning buildings or capturing horses.

McNeill's Rangers were quite effective and soon became the scourge of the Union. In April of 1863, the rangers raided a union camp and captured 12 soldiers, five wagons, and 25 horses. In June, they captured an entire fort, and later they stole 740 head of sheep, 160 cattle, and 40 horses. All of the animals were turned over to Confederate generals to be used for food for the Southern army.

Supplying the Confederates with food was an important job. The Northern blockades had stopped shipment of goods to the South, and many of the Confederate soldiers lived in near starvation conditions. McNeill and his rangers were literally keeping the army fed and alive.

One of McNeill's greatest successes was leading his rangers on a raid of the Baltimore and Ohio railroad. With just 60 men, McNeill was able to seize the Piedmont garrison, cut all of the telegraph lines, and capture a B&O Locomotive. They burned the rail lines and destroyed the machine shops that serviced the trains. They also stranded thousands of Union soldiers who could no longer use the B&O rail line.

Union General Kelly was furious. McNeill's Rangers had nearly run his soldiers out of the area. Kelly put out orders to stop McNeill's Rangers and kill their leader.

But McNeill was not done tormenting the Union: One afternoon his rangers happened upon a group of Union soldiers who were swimming nude in the South Branch River. The rangers charged on the soldiers and captured all of them without firing a shot.

McNeill and his rangers continued capturing soldiers, animals, and weapons for the Confederacy until November of 1864. At that time McNeill died of wounds suffered in a raid. But his rangers lived on, led by his son, Lieutenant Jesse McNeill. Well-taught by his father, the younger McNeill continued to lead raids, capturing more food, weapons, and ammunition for the Confederacy. The rangers only disbanded after General Robert E. Lee's surrender on April 9, 1865.

ATTACK ON THE ALBEMARLE

Battle between the *Sassacus* and the *Albemarle*, May 1864

The CSS *Albemarle* was the terror of Union troops. The Confederate ironclad ship had successfully rammed and sunk the USS *Southfield*. It had severely damaged the USS *Miami* and was responsible for 2,800 Union soldiers surrendering to the Confederates. Something had to be done.

Navy commanders formulated a plan, and then called on Lieutenant William Cushing. The young lieutenant had earned a reputation for leading daring raids on the Confederates, but now he was to be given his toughest assignment yet: attack and sink the rebels' strongest ship. Cushing didn't have to think twice—his good friend had been the captain of the USS *Miami* and had been killed in the fight. Cushing said he would do whatever it took to sink the *Albemarle*.

Cushing was sent to New York to learn about the navy's new steam launches. These were small maneuverable boats outfitted with torpedoes. These Civil War torpedoes were more like a modern-day bomb. Cushing would have to get close enough to the CSS *Albemarle* to throw the torpedo onto the ship. The torpedo was attached to a wire line. Once the torpedo had been thrown, a tug on the line would cause it to explode. It was dangerous and would require a great deal of skill to throw the torpedo and set it off without killing himself or damaging his own ship. Cushing practiced until he felt that he could meet the challenge. Then, he gathered his crew.

Cushing started the mission with two steam launches, but as they were traveling through the Chesapeake Bay, one of the launches was captured by Confederates. Cushing and the crew of the remaining boat decided to go ahead with their mission.

"Impossibilities are for the timid," Cushing later commented. "We determined to overcome all obstacles."

Under the cover of heavy rain, Cushing and his crew came within a few hundred yards of the *Albemarle* before they were spotted by the Confederates. But as soon as Cushing's ship was seen, shouts went up and guns started firing.

The *Albemarle* had been damaged in its previous fights and was being repaired. It was heavily guarded. Shots came from the guns of the *Albemarle* and from the shore. Shots came so close to Cushing that they tore through his coat. But he stood steady in the launch until he could get close enough to throw the torpedo onto the *Albemarle*.

Shots rained down around Cushing as he threw the torpedo with one hand and held the firing line in his other. He tossed the torpedo, felt it land on the *Albemarle*, then pulled the line. The torpedo exploded and shook both boats so hard

READ ALL ABOUT IT!

Newspaper boys were a common sight in both Union and Confederate army camps. Newspapers were the major form of information for soldiers. Newspaper boys had free access to both camps and were often asked for information about what they saw and heard in the opposing camps. These 9- and 10-year-old boys were some of the youngest spies in the Civil War.

that men fell into the water. Cushing yelled to his crewmates to save themselves, and he dove into the water.

Cushing swam for shore, but the swift current of the Roanoke River carried him downstream. He couldn't see what happened. Had he sunk the ship? Had his men survived?

He reached the shore and rested in some tall weeds. He heard men walking near him and tried to stay quiet and hidden. They were Confederate soldiers discussing the sinking of the ship. Cushing and his crew had been successful. They had saved the Union from the most deadly ironclad the Confederates had built.

SPY TRAINING

Tracking Practice

Tracking is when you look for signs of where a person or animal has moved. Tracking is an important part of spy work and can be very difficult, so it takes a lot of practice. When you are tracking a person, you need to look for clues like footprints in wet soil or sand or broken branches and sticks or flattened grass where a person has walked. To practice tracking, you will need a partner and a few simple tools.

Materials:

- ❑ Prize to hide— something simple like a ball or small stuffed animal
- ❑ Magnifying glass
- ❑ A spy partner

Tell your partner to hide the "prize" somewhere in your yard or in a park. Give your partner 10 to 20 seconds, just like you would in a game of hide and seek. After you have finished counting, see if you can track your spy partner's movements.

Use your magnifying glass to look for clues such as smashed grass and footprints. Think about how far he could have gone in the time you gave him. See how quickly you can find the "prize." Then give your partner a chance to practice his skills.

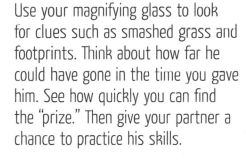

Ranger Camp

Being a ranger in the Civil War required good physical stamina and some great skills at being sneaky. The rangers had to be able to hide outside and blend in with the bushes and trees. Sometimes they had to crawl to get from one hiding place to another. They also had to use leaves and sticks to camouflage themselves.

You can set up your own ranger training camp for your friends. You just need a good outdoor space, some leaves, grass, and the supervision of an adult.

Materials:

- ❏ Leaves
- ❏ Grass
- ❏ Mud or dirt
- ❏ Old clothes
- ❏ Masking tape
- ❏ Permission from an adult

Give yourself a ranger disguise by sticking leaves and grass to your shirt and hat. Hide your face with a light covering of mud. Make sure you do NOT put mud or dirt by your eyes or mouth. Once you are disguised, you are ready for ranger drills.

Army Crawl

Set a starting point and a finish line. Crawl from one end to the other on your stomach. You cannot rise up onto your hands and knees or you are out of the race.

Camouflage Practice

Play this ranger game like a game of hide and seek, except the objective is to blend in with the trees and bushes around you. Select one person to be the seeker. Have the other rangers hide themselves outdoors. As the seeker starts to look for you, you must try to sneak back to base without being caught. You may need to run from bush to bush to avoid being seen. The best rangers will not get caught by the seeker.

TARGET PRACTICE

Materials:
- ❏ Old sheet or blanket
- ❏ Filled water balloons
- ❏ Permanent marker

Use the marker to draw a bull's-eye in the center of the sheet. Divide your rangers into two teams. Give each team the same number of water balloons. Have them line up. Lay the sheet on the ground about 20 feet away from the ranger teams. Have each team member practice hitting the target with the water balloon. The team with the most bull's-eyes wins. They are ready to be rangers. Keep practicing until all of the rangers can hit the bull's-eye.

Col. William H. Telford and officers, 50th Regiment Pennsylvania Infantry at Fort Craig, Arlington, VA

BIBLIOGRAPHY

BOOKS AND PUBLICATIONS

Bonansinga, J. (2012). *Pinkerton's war: The Civil War's greatest spy and the birth of the U.S. Secret Service.* Guilford, CT: Globe Pequot Press.

Byko, M. (2001). Raising the Hunley: Archaeology meets technology. *Journal of the Minerals, Metals, & Materials Society, 53*(3), 12–14. Retrieved from http://www.tms.org/pubs/journals/JOM/0103/Byko-0103.html

Carter, A. R. (2009). *The sea eagle: The Civil War memoir of Lt. Cdr. William B. Cushing U.S.N.* Lanham, MD: Rowman & Littlefield.

Davis, B. (1996). *The Civil War: Strange and fascinating facts.* Wings Books.

Hall, R. (1993). *Patriots in disguise: Women warriors of the Civil War.* St. Paul, MN: Paragon House.

Kelly, B. C. (1998). *Best little stories from the Civil War.* Nashville, TN: Cumberland House.

Kelly, B. C. (2001). *Best little stories from the Civil War.* Cumberland House.

Markle, D. E. (1994). *Spies and spymasters of the Civil War.* New York, NY: Hippocrene Books.

Olsen, C. J. (2006). *The American Civil War—A hands-on history.* New York, NY: Farrar, Straus and Giroux.

Pierce, J., & Jukes, P. (2012). Amy went to war with her husband, lived to fight as Richard Anderson. *The Kentucky Civil War Bugle, 6*(4). Retrieved from http://www.thekentuckycivilwarbugle.com/2012-4Qpages/amyclarke.html

Pincock, S. (2006). *Codebreaker: The history of codes and ciphers.* New York, NY: Walker and Company.

Robertson, J. (2013). *The untold Civil War: Exploring the human side of war.* Washington, DC: National Geographic.

Time Life Books. (1985). *Spies, scouts and raiders—Irregular operations.* Alexandria, VA: Author.

Van Doren Stern, P. (1987). *Secret missions of the Civil War.* Santa Barbara, CA: Praeger.

WEBSITES

Adams, N. (2013). *10 strange Civil War weapons.* Retrieved from http://listverse.com/2013/05/02/10-strange-civil-war-weapons/

Central Intelligence Agency. (2009). *A look back . . . the Black Dispatches: Intelligence during the Civil War.* Retrieved from https://www.cia.gov/news-information/featured-story-archive/black-dispatches.html

CivilWarTraveler.com. (2014). *Northern Georgia: Andrews raid (The great locomotive chase).* Retrieved from http://

www.civilwartraveler.com/WEST/GA/nw-Andrews Raid.html

Civil War Trust. (n.d.). *John Singleton Mosby.* Retrieved from http://www.civilwar.org/education/history/biographies/john-singleton-mosby.html

DeMarco, M. (2014). Elizabeth Van Lew (1818–1900). In *Encyclopedia Virginia.* Retrieved from http://encyclopediavirginia.org/van_lew_elizabeth_l_1818-1900

FiddlersGreen.net. (n.d.). *Thaddeus Lowe and his Civil War observation balloon.* Retrieved from http://www.fiddlersgreen.net/models/aircraft/Balloon-Lowe.html

Firearms History, Technology, and Development. (2012). *Harmonica gun/slide gun.* Retrieved from http://firearmshistory.blogspot.com/2012/09/harmonica-gunslide-gun.html

Fold3 by Ancestry.com. (2012). *Battle of Hampton Roads.* Retrieved from http://spotlights.fold3.com/2012/03/07/battle-of-hampton-roads/

Greely, A. W. (n.d.). *The signal corps.* Retrieved from http://www.civilwarsignals.org/pages/signal/signal.html

History Channel. (2014). *American Civil War history: Civil War biological warfare.* Retrieved from http://www.history.com/topics/american-civil-war/american-civil-war-history/videos/civil-war-biological-warfare

Holland, J. J. (2011). Slaves, freedmen: Civil War's forgotten spies. *NBC News.* Retrieved from http://www.nbcnews.com/id/43461045/ns/us_news-life/t/slaves-freedmen-civil-wars-forgotten-spies/#.U8WbQI1dxWF

House Divided: The Civil War Research Engine at Dickinson College. (2007). *John Hanson McNeill.* Retrieved from http://hd.housedivided.dickinson.edu/node/6243

The Jessie Scouts. (2007). Retrieved from http://www.jessiescouts.com/Jessie%20Scouts%20Home.html

Lamb, J. (n.d.). *Mythbusters episode 93 "Confederate steam gun" features Winans steam gun*. Retrieved from http://www.2ndmdinfantryus.org/winans.html

Library of Congress, Science Reference Services. (2011). *Civil War aeronautics (1861–1865)*. Retrieved from http://www.loc.gov/rr/scitech/SciRefGuides/civilwar aeronautics.html

Lincoln and the telegraph. (n.d.). Retrieved from http://www.bekkahwalker.net/comt111a/websites_11/liang_site/historical_uses.html

Missouri State Parks. (n.d.). *Fort Davidson state historic site*. Retrieved from http://mostateparks.com/park/fort-davidson-state-historic-site

Mythbusters. (2007). *Steam machine gun*. Retrieved from https://www.youtube.com/watch?v=YKhLgPyymfU

National Archives. (n.d.). *Rose O'Neal Greenhow*. Retrieved from http://www.archives.gov/research/military/civil-war/greenhow.html

National Women's History Museum. (n.d.). *Belle Boyd (1844–1900)*. Retrieved from http://www.nwhm.org/education-resources/biography/biographies/belle-boyd/

Naval Historical Center. (1999). *CSS Albemarle*. Retrieved from http://www.history.navy.mil/photos/sh-us-cs/csa-sh/csash-ag/albmrl.htm

Naval History & Heritage Command. (n.d.). *H. L. Hunley, Confederate submarine*. Retrieved from http://www.history.navy.mil/branches/org12-3.htm

Pinkerton Consulting and Investigations. (2013). *History*. Retrieved from http://www.pinkerton.com/history

The Southern Museum. (n.d.). *The General locomotive and the great locomotive chase*. Retrieved from http://www.southernmuseum.org/exhibits/the-general/

To the Sound of Guns. (2013). *"Bright, silvery rays upon our front": Use of the calcium light against Battery Wagner*.

Retrieved from http://markerhunter.wordpress.com/2013/09/05/calcium-light-battery-wagner/

Weaver, M. (2012). *Lafayette Baker.* Retrieved from http://www.americancivilwarstory.com/lafayette-baker.html

Weaver, M. (2012). *Timothy Webster.* Retrieved from http://www.americancivilwarstory.com/timothy-webster.html

ABOUT THE
AUTHOR

Stephanie Bearce is a writer, a teacher, and a history detective. She loves tracking down spies and uncovering secret missions from the comfort of her library in St. Charles, MO. When she isn't writing or teaching, Stephanie loves to travel the world and go on adventures with her husband, Darrell.

More Books in This Series

TOP SECRET FILES

Stealthy spies, secret weapons, and special missions are just part of the mysteries uncovered when kids dare to take a peek at the *Top Secret Files*. Featuring books that focus on often unknown aspects of history, this series is sure to hook even the most reluctant readers, taking them on a journey as they try to unlock some of the secrets of our past.

Top Secret Files: The American Revolution

George Washington had his own secret agents, hired pirates to fight the British, and helped Congress smuggle weapons, but you won't learn that in your history books! Learn the true stories of the American Revolution and how spies used musket balls, books, and laundry to send messages. Discover the female Paul Revere, solve a spy puzzle, and make your own disappearing ink. It's all part of the true stories from the *Top Secret Files: The American Revolution*.

ISBN-13: 978-1-61821-247-4

Top Secret Files: World War I

Flame throwers, spy trees, bird bombs, and Hell Fighters were all a part of World War I, but you won't learn that in your history books! Uncover long-lost secrets of spies like Howard Burnham, "The One Legged Wonder," and nurse-turned-spy, Edith Cavell. Peek into secret files to learn the truth about the Red Baron and the mysterious Mata Hari. Then learn how to build your own Zeppelin balloon and mix up some invisible ink. It's all part of the true stories from the *Top Secret Files: World War I*.

ISBN-13: 978-1-61821-241-2

Top Secret Files: World War II

Spy school, poison pens, exploding muffins, and Night Witches were all a part of World War II, but you won't learn that in your history books! Crack open secret files and read about the mysterious Ghost Army, rat bombs, and doodlebugs. Discover famous spies like the White Mouse, super-agent Garbo, and baseball player and spy, Moe Berg. Then build your own secret agent kit and create a spy code. It's all part of the true stories from the *Top Secret Files: World War II*.

ISBN-13: 978-1-61821-244-3